Information Technology Roadmap
For Professional Service Firms

By P.J. Colbeck

PERSPECTIVE SHIFTS PRESS
Canton, MI

Book design and cover illustration / **Gabi Schmidt** (www.gabischmidt.com)

Editing / **Bridget Travers**

Illustrations / **John Romans** of techMedia Design (www.techmediadesign.com)

Printing / **Dickinson Press**

Perspective Shifts Press
P.O. Box 871623
Canton, MI 48187
info@perspectiveshifts.biz

Library of Congress Cataloging-in-Publication Data
Colbeck, P. J. (Patrick J.)
Information technology roadmap for professional service firms / by P.J. Colbeck.
p. cm.
Includes bibliographical references and index.
LCCN 2006930286
ISBN 0-9785049-0-9

1. Small business--Management. 2. Small business--Electronic Information resources--Management. 3. Information technology--Management. I. Title.

HD62.7.C635 2006 658.02'2
QBI06-600293

"To my wife, Angie…

your love, faith, and wisdom make each day with you better than the day before."

P.J.

Acknowledgements

I want to express sincere appreciation for all of the people who have lent their considerable talents to help launch or execute my first book project. Without the comforting assistance of the following individuals, this book would not have been possible:

Harry Brelsford
Bob Orlowski
Anne Stanton
Brent Leary
Naseem Saab
Jesse Shiah
Bridget Travers
Gabi Schmidt
John Romans
Jeri Butler
Startup Nation Community Forum
Nora Gessert
Ian Radcliff
Mike Martin
Kathleen Barcroft
Jim Crossman
Bob Schmidt
Christine Buonocore
Alban de Bergevin
Rudi van den Berg
Dan Kocun
Ed Martin

...and last, but not least, all of my immediate family, my in-laws, and my church family. The roadmap for this project has been long and arduous at times, but God has blessed me with the right people at the right times to help smooth out the bumps along the way.

Preface

Ah…the promise of Information Technology – speed, efficiency, and that special feeling of satisfaction you have when you know the rest of the business world is not racing past you on the information superhighway.

Sounds nice in theory, but most small business owners don't have time to put a key into the ignition of any vehicle that might get them onto this route. Once they finally do take the plunge on a vehicle for the information superhighway, they often find that the manual for just one of the vehicle components competes for size with your local phone directory. To top it off, once they get onto the information superhighway, they find that folks are constantly changing the technology road signs, making it difficult to find your way to the land of speed, efficiency, and special satisfaction.

The purpose of this book is to provide small business owners with a pocket-sized roadmap that you can take with you on your journey into the underutilized world of IT value.

The purpose of this book is to provide small business owners with a pocket-sized roadmap that you can take with you on your journey into the underutilized world of IT value. There is a deliberate attempt to print this IT roadmap in the language of your business and not the cryptic, ever-evolving language of IT jargon. If you prefer to add supercalifragilisticinexpealidocious IT terms to your business vocabulary, several excellent resources for folks who speak IT are referenced in the book for your pursuit.

This book is focused first and foremost on the application of IT as a means to improve your business as opposed to IT being an end in and of itself. The best IT solution in the world will not be effective in helping you shape your business unless you have a basic understanding of how you would like to manage your business. All computers help you to do is to execute ineffective processes with more speed – plus more potential for disaster. This book seeks to arm you with the right questions and point you toward the right answers specific to your business.

The IT Roadmap begins by prompting ▶

readers to describe their business in terms that make it easier to determine how IT solutions might be useful to their business. The **"What do you do?"** section addresses your specific needs in the Professional Services Industry. This section applies a broad brush to the industry and analyzes the strengths, weaknesses, opportunities, and threats associated with typical Professional Service Firms. This assessment provides the business backdrop that is an essential first step in the development of an effective IT strategy.

The **"How do you do do it?"** section will help you bridge the communication gap between your business and technology providers. The book provides the reader with a means of capturing and communicating information about his or her business in a way that will give solution providers in the often strange world of technology the information they need to help get you where you need to go. It will also provide you with a tangible business model that will be useful independent of your exploration of Information Technology. This passport to the world of IT features key information about how you conduct business, including key packets of information that you pass back and forth within your company and amongst your customers and suppliers. These packets of information are organized in the language and customs of the technology world. This passport should provide you with a convenient reference for improving your business operations with or without technology.

Have you ever found yourself lost while traveling in a strange city or even when wandering around in a strange building? One of the most comforting sights you might find is a map featuring a reassuring "You are Here" symbol. Wouldn't it be nice to start your journey on the information superhighway with a similar marker? The **"Where is your business today?"** section of the book provides you with tools that help you to find your position on the IT Roadmap. It maps out the scorecard and key performance indicators that help gauge the effectiveness of your business operations. Once you understand where you are, you will be better equipped to make decisions about IT investments. If you don't know where you are, finding your destination will be very difficult.

Speaking of destination, the next section of the book covers **"Where do you want your business to be?"** This section defines ways that readers can produce a clear, tangible profile of their business destinations. Using the information gained about your business in previous sections, we target the most important areas of your business operations and organize them into "value streams". These value streams provide the means of establishing realistic targets or objectives for your business.

Once you know where you are and you've defined where you want to go, the IT Roadmap provides you with practical tools and guidelines to help you map out a path to your destination in the "**How are you going to get your business there?**" section. This section begins with an overview of how to define a practical strategy to meet your objectives and then shifts gears into how to execute that strategy using the best practices of Project Management. By the end of the section, you will have a handle on the timing, costs and benefits associated with deploying one or more IT products.

The book attempts to consolidate the latest thinking and best practices of multiple disciplines into a single, integrated, practical guide. Professionals familiar with Value Stream Management, Six Sigma Analysis and Design, Business Process Engineering, Business Performance Measurement, Enterprise Project Management, as well as those with technical backgrounds in IT should find some familiar themes within these pages. Even if you are coming across these topics for the first time, don't worry. The book has also simplified these topics so that they are easy to apply in the development of your very own IT Roadmap.

Table of Contents

XML
AHEAD
ENTER
TCP/IP
SPOKEN
HERE
Upgrade
Microsoft
Office
Small Business Edition 2003
556-0210

INTRODUCTION

"If you do not know where you are going, any road will take you there".

(Chesire Cat, *Alice in Wonderland*)

The world of information technology is uncharted territory for many small businesses. While many budding entrepreneurs have peered into this territory, very few of them are comfortable venturing beyond the borders of their personal technology comfort zone. Even fewer have a defined strategy or "roadmap" for exploring this "Unknown Territory" and making permanent settlements.

Why do so many small businesses hesitate to venture far into the land of information technology?

- They don't speak the same language...(XML, ASP, ISP, VPN, HTML).
- The exchange rate or return on investment is unknown.
- The street signs seem to change frequently.
- They are perfectly happy where they are.
- They have no compelling vision of why it needs to be explored.
- IT can be expensive.

Ironically, the natives in the land of information technology have not felt compelled to venture far into the general domain of small businesses until relatively recently. Why are IT providers hesitant to establish trade with small businesses?

- The exchange rate is unfavorable. The cost of sales is similar to the cost of sales for larger companies but the potential revenue opportunity is lower. As a result, IT vendors prefer to seek bigger fish.
- Small business have few people who speak their language – larger organizations have entire departments of IT specialists. Small businesses will often have someone designated as "it" when it comes to dealing with IT issues, but typically they are cornered into playing the part. As a result of these situations, IT vendors often spend a significant amount of time providing what they see as free training.

This book holds that compelling reasons to improve trade between small businesses and IT vendors are many. According to Microsoft, 40 million small businesses operate globally. A market this large does tend to grab the attention of industry. IT vendors are slowly starting to overcome initial hesitancies and increase the attention they pay to small businesses in the ▶

form of increased marketing dollars and the development of products and services tailored to small businesses. To entice small businesses, IT offers significant potential to improve financial performance as well as the quality of life for workers. The internet and mobile communications have become ubiquitous elements of life, yet they only scratch the surface of the capabilities that go along with embracing IT.

Large companies have long benefited from IT as a means of connecting cubicle-bound employees dispersed across the country and globe. A large variety of software solutions are out on the market in response to the needs of larger companies. More often than not, though, these companies require expensive, customized solutions that work around the particular idiosyncrasies of the organization and processes around which the company has morphed. In this, small businesses have a distinct advantage over larger companies. Models of their business operations are much simpler. Professional Service Firms in particular tend to focus on differentiating themselves on the delivery of their services and keep the remainder of their business operations standard. Since software is essentially nothing more than codified process, it follows that their software needs are simpler as well. This represents a significant opportunity for small businesses to reap the fruits of the software solutions developed for the big boys. If the core processes can be kept fairly simple, small businesses will be able to improve the efficiency of their business operations without the need for expensive, customized software solutions. The key to reaping this dividend is to understand how your business really works. Armed with this understanding, you will have the ability to make effective decisions about the direction of your company – and about the direction of your IT infrastructure in particular. If done well, you won't have to rely upon obscure metrics such as IT spending as percentage of revenue to establish or defend your IT budget. You will be able to zero in on metrics specific to your business operations.

This book is focused on Professional Service Firms so that your construction of an IT Roadmap features mile markers that are written in a language managers in these firms recognize. The processes, metrics, and guidance are tailored to the terms found in Professional Service Firms. To begin, let's go over a few key concepts we will come across during our journey: Information, Technology, and Roadmap.

Information

All too often, discussions of Information Technology focus on the technology and practically ignore the information. The key to deploying an effective IT solution is to understand what information one needs to run the business prior to defining the technology that will be deployed. Too often, businesses are distracted by technological "shiny objects" and find themselves experiencing buyer's remorse a few years later. In order to reduce the risk of buyer's remorse, it is important to have a solid understanding of the information that keeps your business engine running. Information is power. Specifically, it is the power to make informed decisions. **Table 1** provides a sample of decisions that you might need to make for your business. Once you understand what decisions you need to make, you can figure out what ▶

Collect information with a purpose
Information for the sake of information is not good information.

Table 1 / Typical Professional Service Firm Decisions

Decision	Information
Which clients should receive the most attention from our staff?	Income and Expense report sorted by client
What training is required by a new hire?	List of skills required by new hires Model of how new hires are currently trained
Should we provide flex time benefits for our employees?	List of who is working on what List of which tasks require collaboration Model of how these tasks are associated with other tasks
How can we improve collaboration with our clients?	List of information needed by our clients List of how this information is typically provided to clients Model of how we manage client relationships
How can we reduce the administrative burden of our most valuable staff members?	List of administrative tasks Time study for each administrative task Reports citing how often they fail to complete an administrative task and what this failure costs our business

Figure 1 Decision-based Information Framework

information you need to effectively make those decisions. Once you know what information you need, you can figure out how to get that information in a regular, reliable manner by documenting the standard processes that govern your daily business operations. Once you identify these processes, you can analyze these processes to see if and where tools might be able to make the executing of these processes more efficient and effective. Do you have the processes and tools in place to help you answer these questions?

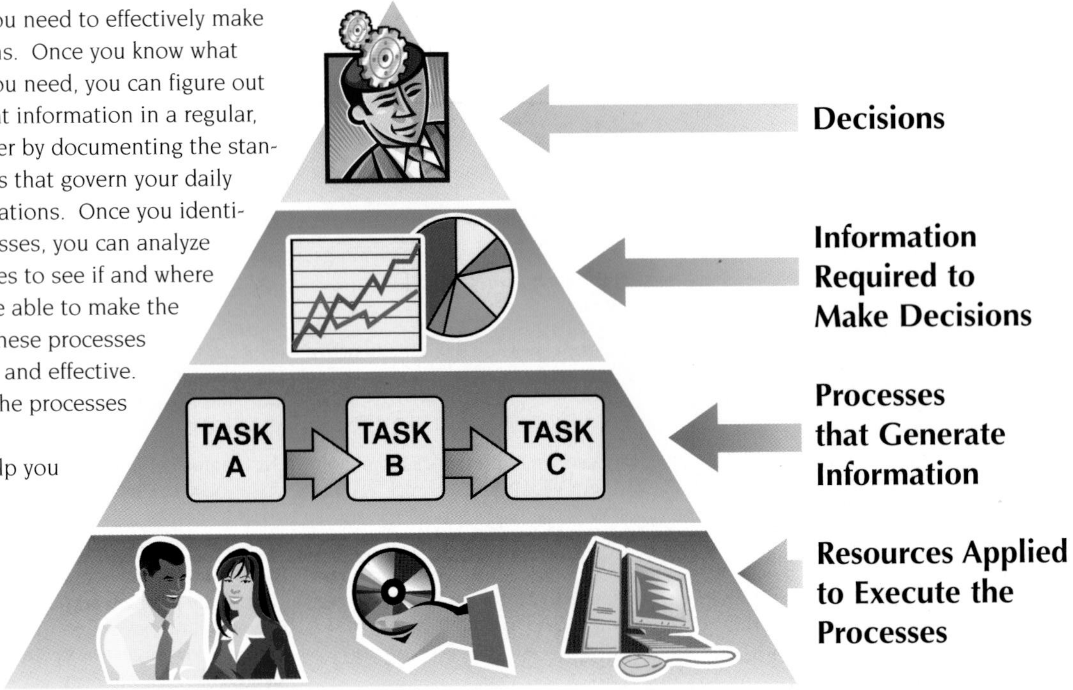

TASK A
TASK B
TASK C

Decisions

Information Required to Make Decisions

Processes that Generate Information

Resources Applied to Execute the Processes

Technology

The tools of this new discipline are the "technology" half of the IT acronym. If these tools do not present information in a manner that supports effective decision making, buyer's remorse is certain. How can technology help a business whose primary asset is its people, such as a Professional Services Firm? The Professional Services Industry is focused on people – the knowledge they have and the skills they have in conveying that knowledge. How effectively do you use that people-based information? Does that information disappear from the company as soon as an employee retires or quits? How do you preserve the reputation of your firm and ensure the quality of the information provided to your clients when new hires are assigned to service them?

The fundamental benefit of Information Technology for any type of organization is that it allows you to digitize information – voice, data, currency, even thoughts – then manipulate that information in the ebb and flow of your business operations. In and of itself, this amounts to a cute parlor trick. However, the true value of digital information as portrayed in **Figure 2** is the flexibility and transportability it provides you in analyzing information to make business decisions. Gutenberg's printing press was not revolutionary because it printed books; books had been created for many centuries before Gutenberg. The printing press was revolutionary because it "digitized" language. Bulky engraving plates, featuring an arrangement of text that was often only good for one use, were replaced by a reusable character set that could be rearranged time and time again to create a unique message. When a member of your staff jots down the number of billable hours dedicated to a specific client, it must be linked to other information about your client and your billing rates to generate an invoice. That same piece of information can also be used to drive a report on total billable hours per employee and drive the numbers that go into your tax returns. All of this linking could be done with an army of clerks, or it could be performed with the judicious application of the latest in information technology.

Figure 2 Digital Promise

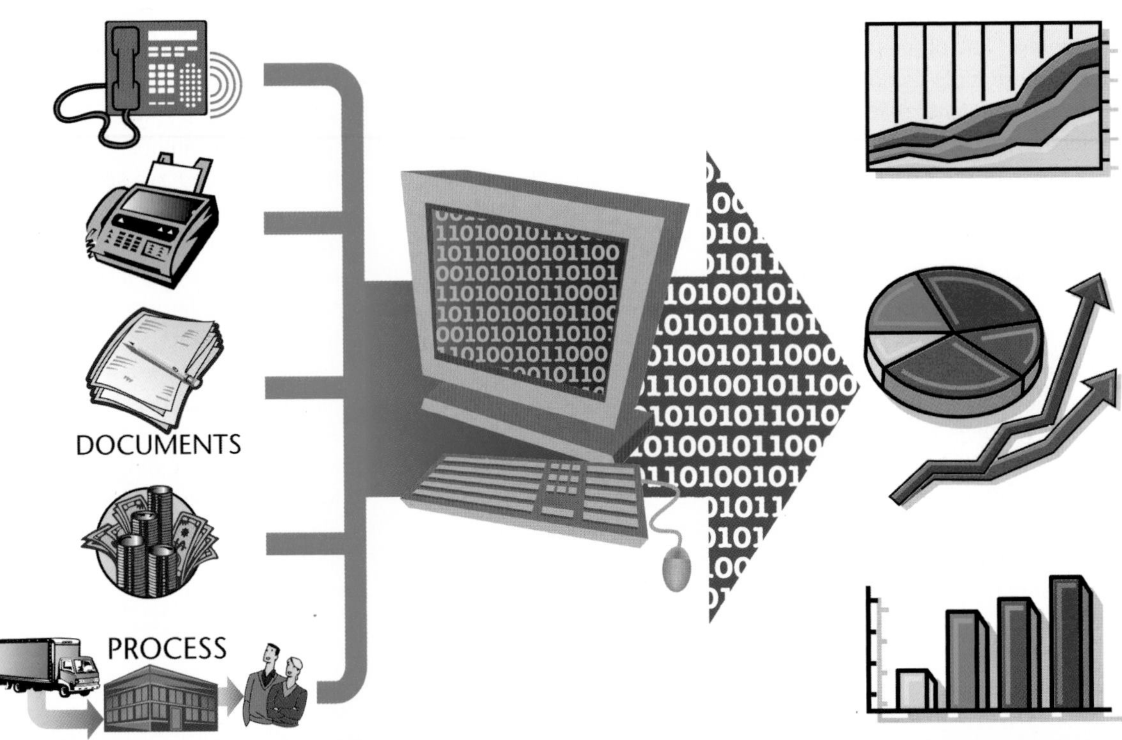

So, let's flash forward from a discussion of revolutionary 15th-century information technology to an overview of the latest trends in information technology....

- **Mobility:** Information has busted beyond the confines of paper. People can access almost any information from almost anywhere in the world and beyond.
- **Security:** While all of this information can be accessible by anyone, anywhere in the world, not all of it should be. Information technology is increasingly focused on securing this wealth of information.
- **Flexibility:** Software has evolved beyond "one-size-fits-all" all product offerings towards an increased emphasis on "configurable" solutions. Configurable software provides business users with little IT knowledge the capability to configure the software to reflect their needs and preferences. In the past, the process of aligning software with the business required costly and risky customization of standard software packages. Large, feature-laden programs are being replaced by smaller, task-based applications.
- **Standardization:** The basic "nuts and bolts" of software programs (e.g. search routines, security applets, etc.) are taking the route already taken by the actual nuts and bolts found at your local hardware store. Many of the components of software programs are being standardized as a means of expediting software development and improving the quality of software.
- **Interoperability:** Information created in one program can increasingly be shared with other programs, even programs hosted on a different platform (e.g. Mac or Windows). Enterprise Information Infrastructure software is coming onto the market to help connect all of the information that you depend upon to run your business independent of the source of that information.
- **Simplicity:** If you are comfortable surfing the web, you should be comfortable with the latest trends in software user interfaces. The lines between surfing for information on the internet and manipulating information on your hard drive will be blurred. In addition, applications are increasingly being designed to work the way you think. Software is being developed around models of your business processes rather than forcing you to model your business after the technology.

In order to define an effective Information Technology strategy based on these trends, it is important to understand that information technology is much more than what appears to the naked eye. The user interface ▶

Platform Politics

As with many strange lands, the world of IT is ripe with political factions. These factions are aligned with the principle software platforms or operating systems that are out there... **Windows (Microsoft), Mac OS (Apple),** and **Linux (Open Source).** Microsoft is the current ruling party on the basis of people voting with their dollars. Apple is the media darling that gets a lot of air time, but has trouble generating enough dollar votes to warrant support from the software development lobby. The Open Source faction is rather anti-establishment, believing that free software ranks right up there with the Bill of Rights. Microsoft is squarely in the crosshairs of its competitors and a large segment of the IT professional community that prefers diversity in the market. Before you select a core platform for your business, make sure that you separate politics from the needs of your business.

(See Figure 3) is only the tip of the iceberg in the realm of what needs to work in order to get information to the monitor on your computer. When you look at an email message from within the web browser software on your laptop, the information in the message was actually pulled from a database on an email server. In order for you to access that server, you need to have access to the network that hosts that server and have a pointer on your desktop to the specific address of that server. While you chose to view the email message from within your web browser, you could have also viewed the same message from within a specialized mail program such as Microsoft Outlook.

Figure 3 Inside Software

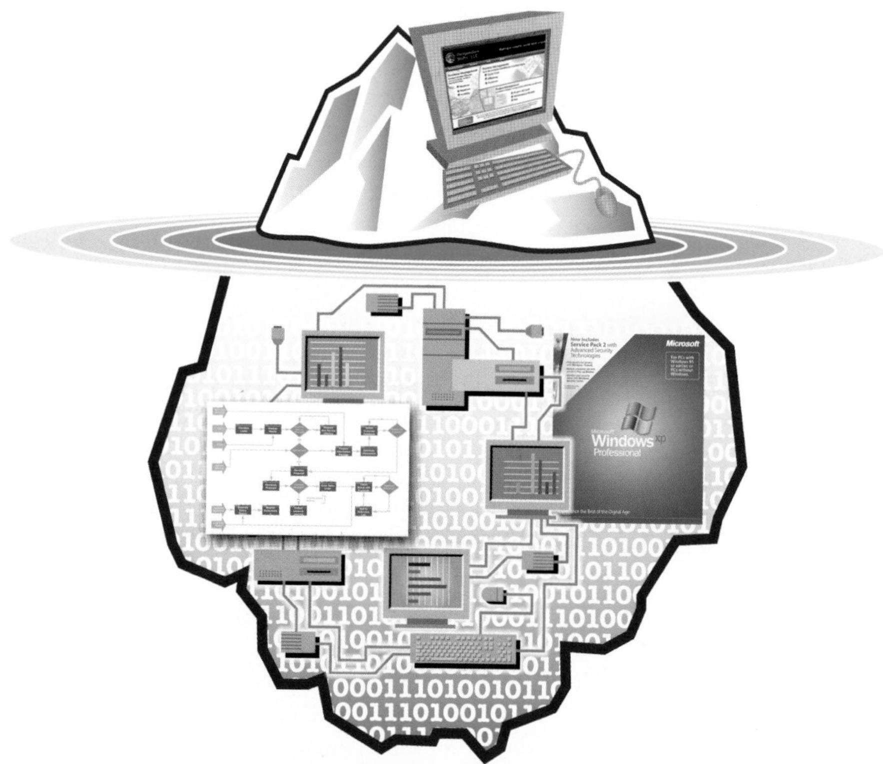

For many users, the window into the world of software is the hardware on which the software is installed. When a new laptop ships, it typically comes pre-installed with a generous suite of software programs. Personal Digital Assistants (PDA) such as iPAQs or Blackberrys include powerful software applications in a pint size package. Even cell phones are providing more and more exposure to software. These portals of entry into the world of technology are just the start. Typically, hardware is simply an enabler for software to do its thing. Software controls the movement of information and this will be the focus of the remainder of the book.

The following general technology guidelines should help prepare you for your excursions into the world of information technology:

- **Digitize** your information to improve the flexibility you have in regards to how you operate your business.
- **Centralize** your information to improve the access to your information by multiple employees and/or software programs.
- **Secure** your information so that only the people that need to see it can see it.
- **Standardize** on a single platform in order to maximize the ease and efficiency of ensuring interoperability between software programs.

If you follow these guidelines, you have covered the basics of a technology-driven strategy. However, this strategy alone will not provide you with the full bang for the buck potential of information technology. For this, we need to take a much more scenic journey.

Roadmap

You can design your business around technology or design your technology around your business. The friction between business and IT in most large corporations can be traced to this dilemma. This book aims to provide you with the tools to take the latter route in style and with performance.

The roadmap outlined in this book will enable you to make effective connections between the key components of your business. **Figure 4** shows how management often finds itself at the center of what can be a complex juggling act. You will find that it is risky business to make decisions about any one of the areas in **Figure 4** without considering the impacts to the others. Without an understanding of how they tie together, this can be a very challenging exercise.

Figure 4 Complex Connections

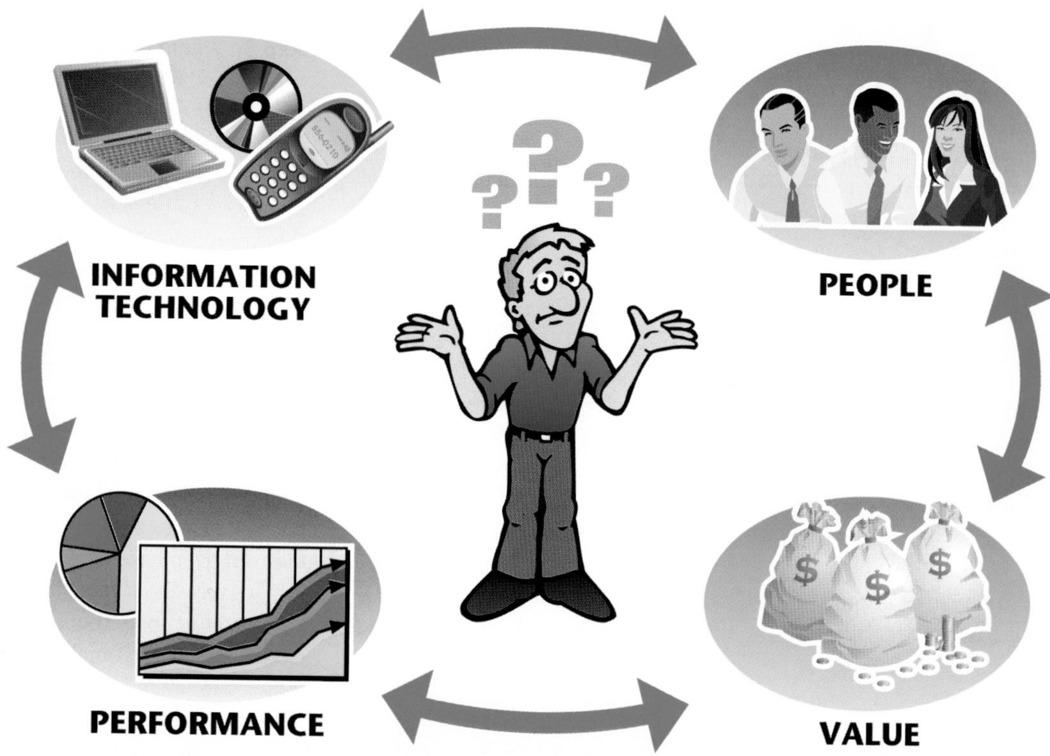

The IT Roadmap produced by following the guidelines in this book will give you the tools necessary to take effective action within the sometimes confusing world of information technology.

Your roadmap will provide you with the following features:

- Understand the connections between your business performance and the people that drive that performance.
- Understand the connections between your business performance and information technology.
- Understand the connections between information technology and the value it provides to your business.

A roadmap is a plan of action. The focus of this roadmap is your business – not the technology. Technology is only introduced as a means of improving your business. It is easy to get distracted by shiny software objects that can veer small businesses into dangerous situations.

Essentially, you can take one of two approaches to generating a plan of action–high risk or low risk. High-risk approaches feature little information and impulsive purchases. Low-risk approaches feature gathering as much information as is necessary to make good decisions and make purchases in accordance with a long term strategy. You don't need a book to take the high-risk approach – all you need is a lot of money and time. If neither of these assets is in ready supply, you may wish to consider the low risk, 5-step approach outlined in this book.

These 5 steps are as follows:

Step 1: What do you do?
Step 2: How do you do it?
Step 3: Where is your business today?
Step 4: Where do you want your business to be?
Step 5: How are you going to get your business there?

This approach is straightforward, but the results can be powerful whether or not you decide to deploy a variety of IT products and services. For your convenience, the key information produced by each step is summarized at the end of each section. With this information, you will effectively move your business forward at your own pace and explore opportunities you may not even have known existed. Before we talk about moving you out of your comfort zone, though, let's take a closer look at what makes you tick.

STEP 1: WHAT DO YOU DO?

"Defining what its task is and what it should not be is the most essential step in making... institutions...manageable, managed, and performing".

Peter F. Drucker, Management Consultant and Writer, *The Changing World of the Executive* (Quadrangle, 1982)

Professional Service Firms are special. They are knowledge organizations. Knowledge organizations generate revenue as a direct result of applying the knowledge of their employees in one or more specialty areas for the benefit of their clients. Your specialty area may be one of the following:

- Financial Services
- Accounting
- Law
- Architecture
- Advertising
- Graphic Design
- Engineering
- Consulting
- Real Estate

SIPOC Models
SIPOC models provide high-level models of the flow of information in an organization (See Glossary)

What does a day in your business life look like? A first glance at your business operations might look something like the model shown in **Figure 5.** You provide services to customers in exchange for revenue. You probably have one or more suppliers in which the direction of this transaction is reversed. Partners typically help out by providing additional sales leads and service delivery that complements the services offered by your company.

In order to get a better understanding of how IT might be able to help a Professional Services Firm, let's take a well-known consultant tool out of our pocket consultant series toolbox – SWOT analysis. SWOT is an acronym for Strengths, Weaknesses, Opportunities and Threats. As you review this SWOT analysis, it is worth pointing out that this same analysis could also apply to significant segments of businesses outside of the Professional Services Firm domain. This analysis is intended to be a general assessment of a typical Professional Service Firm. The specific attributes of your business may vary.

Figure 5 Business SIPOC Model

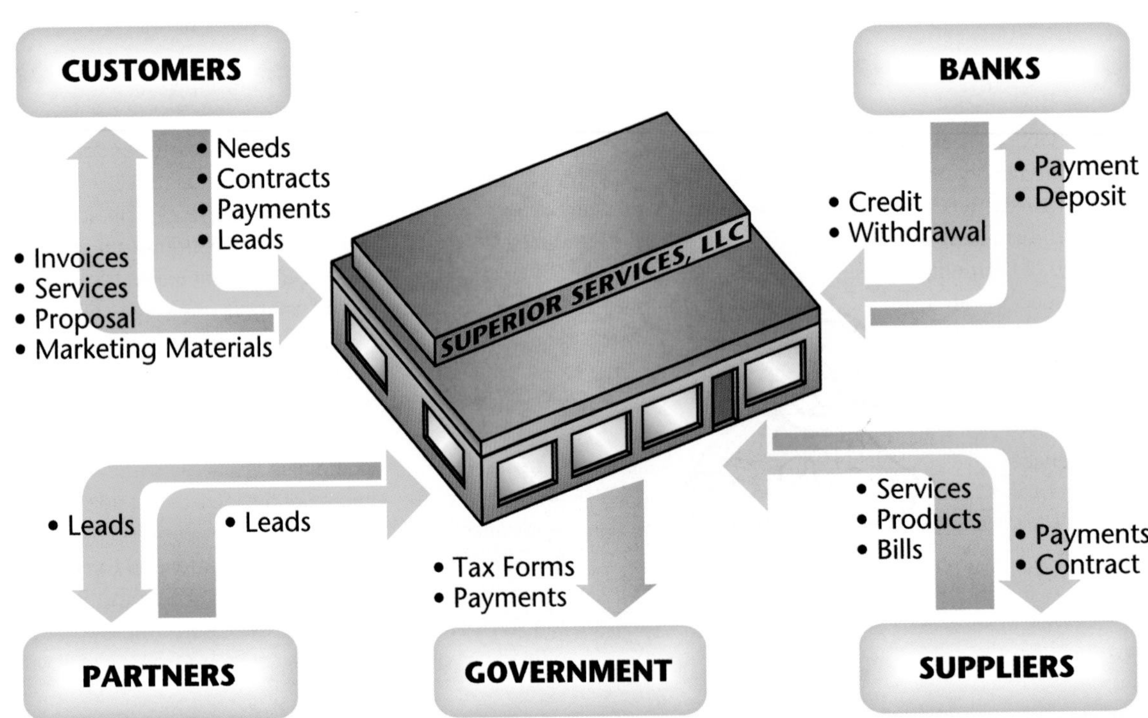

Strengths

A significant number of strengths belong to the Professional Service Firm business model. As business models go, it is relatively straightforward. In exchange for your time, clients pay you. Why doesn't everyone get paid for their time? The simple answer is that you know something that your clients don't know as well as you or don't have the time to apply. This domain knowledge is your principle asset. Since your principle asset is your people, your overhead can be quite low compared to other businesses in the retail or manufacturing sector. While you may own buildings and office equipment, the principle assets of these companies are your employees and their respective intellectual capital. These assets are inherently portable, which corresponds to another significant advantage – the flexibility to service your clients from their offices, your offices or even your employee's home offices. Last but not least, Professional Service Firms typically have very strong relationships with their clients. Often these clients may be friends, friends of a friend, or old co-workers. The relationships you have with your clients are usually very important strengths for your business.

IT can reinforce these strengths in a variety of ways...

What if you could generate revenue from your domain knowledge without having to spend time with clients? Companies such as LegalZoom (legalzoom.com) have found a way to leverage their human capital and package their professional services for the internet consumer.

What if you could share best practices with everyone in the company? This amounts to earning dividends on your intellectual capital. Microsoft SharePoint software provides powerful collaboration capabilities in a package that non-programmers will find easy to use and maintain. In addition to document management, novice users can easily manage surveys, contact information, events, or pretty much anything that you can capture in a spreadsheet. Segments of this knowledge base could also be opened up to clients, partners, or suppliers if desired.

What if you could provide your employees with more flexibility in regards to where they work? Many employees struggle with traffic jams and work-life balance. A robust, secure IT network could provide ▶

employees with opportunities to work from home and still access all of the information and systems they need in order to perform their job effectively.

What if everyone on your staff knew what your clients needed, who talked with them last and what they talked about? Client Relationship Management (CRM) software provides companies with the ability to track communications with clients (emails, phone calls, faxes, etc.) in a centralized database that can be accessed by all employees granted the security rights to do so. These messages can be correlated with the contract opportunities associated with the client and the types of services in which they are interested.

Weaknesses

Professional Service Firms also have their share of weaknesses. The best IT software is no good unless you have folks that know how to deploy it and keep it in good working order. Most Professional Service Firms are not known for their IT proficiency, nor is the vast majority of their employees. While many of your employees may not be tied down to one of your offices, they do tend to be tied down by the need to be present at client offices, either for the duration of their contract or a significant portion thereof. This situation effectively limits the reach of your services to those clients who live within commuting distance of the homes of your employee. In addition to a lack of technical expertise, most Professional Service Firms are not known for their adherence to standard processes or procedures. If you need to get something done within the company, it is often a matter of knowing who to contact, not how to do it. When you extend this situation to your service delivery, you leave the door open to significant variations in service quality and customer dissatisfaction. In many cases, if an employee leaves the company, so does their expertise – be it in service delivery or accounts receivable processing. Oftentimes, when employees leave your company they become your competitors or are hired by your clients, thereby eliminating the need for your services.

IT can lessen the severity of these weaknesses in several ways…

What if you could buy IT proficiency short of hiring IT employees? ▶

If you are hesitant to develop IT proficiency internally, the majority of IT solutions can be implemented by a special class of vendors referred to as a Managed Service Provider. These companies handle all of the headaches associated with purchasing hardware, purchasing software, upgrading software, and keeping your data secure. If you are anxious about having your business information somewhere other than within the four walls of your company, you also have the option of hiring IT service firms such as Computer Troubleshooters to administer your own IT assets at your site – full time or as required.

What if you could extend your service reach globally via the internet? Even if you don't currently have offices around the world, you can capture a lot of information from potential clients if you have the right lure. A good website can be used to capture information about client interests and locations. Even if they are not converted into clients, you can gain valuable information about the marketplace and just maybe where you should open up your next office.

What if you could evaluate what processes were working and which processes weren't? Innovative business process management solutions such as Ascentn's AgilePoint software suite provide business users with the capability to define and monitor the execution of business workflows such as document approval routing. These features are provided using Microsoft Office tools and via your internet web browser.

What if you could maintain copies of all information created by your employees in support of their responsibilities? Infrastructure software such as Microsoft's Small Business Server provides you with the capability of backing up employee My Document folders. This feature can also be used by employees to restore accidentally deleted documents without the need for IT administrator assistance.

Opportunities

There are always opportunities to deliver your services faster, more efficiently, with better quality, and to a broader market. In a business where time is money, it may not readily appear that it would be in the best interest of a Professional Services Firm to deliver their services faster. At second glance, though, many clients will pay a premium for speed (ask any customer of FedEx). Your ability to deliver your initial services quickly and effectively will increase the likelihood that your clients will come to you with more expensive service demands or even retainer agreements. As your engagements become more complex, the ability to manage expectations with the client effectively becomes more difficult. There are always significant opportunities to improve communications with the client, not to mention improving communications internally within your business. A significant opportunity to improve business performance lies in the realm of managing the approval workflows for documents. On the subject of business performance, how do you track it today? There is a significant opportunity to reduce the overhead of report generation and improve the quality of the information in the reports.

What if you could provide your customers with on-demand services? Impulse buyers are not found only in the retail sector. Differentiate between commodity and specialized services. Box up the commodities for the internet and reserve the specialized for your service delivery team. What if you could provide your customers with the ability to track the status of your work for them? Enterprise Project Management solutions such as Microsoft's Project Server can provide web-based access to project status information for internal or external use. Task status can be updated by the personnel responsible for them via familiar software such as Microsoft Outlook. In addition to providing timing status information, the system can also be used to manage the supply and demand for all of your resources. Once you have resources associated with tasks, you will also be able to track the costs and revenue opportunities associated with supporting a given client.

What if you could know the approval status of any document? Collaboration software such as Microsoft Windows Sharepoint Services provides basic workflow management capabilities in addi- ▶

tion to the other communication features of the product. Business Process Management tool suites such as Ascentn's AgilePoint can be used to design more elaborate workflow management processes tailored to your business.

What if you could create an interactive forum for employees at different offices without having to waste time and money traveling to a central location? Microsoft's LiveMeeting service provides you with an easy-to-use video and audio bridge. Sessions can even be archived for later review, making it ideal for on-demand training services.

What if you could eliminate the time that it takes to generate status reports? In addition to many of the built-in capabilities such as those found in Project Server and AgilePoint, Microsoft's Business Scorecard Manager provides the ability to generate reports featuring data from multiple sources (spreadsheets, databases, etc.) into a single, consolidated, web-based report that allows users to drill down into the individual sources of the information.

Threats

Some sharks are circling in the waters for Professional Service Firms content with the status quo. While "Made in China" labels are most prominent on manufactured goods, services are also targets of global competitors. The threat of global outsourcing.is no longer limited to call centers and software programmers. The global reach of the internet has opened up many sectors to this threat, including accounting, legal research, and engineering.

If a process can be defined, it can be outsourced

Another important threat comes from regulatory restrictions. These regulations can be created as a result of industry best practices or government intervention. The Financial Accounting Standards Board and its Generally Accepted Accounting Principles (GAAP) is an example of ▶

an industry-imposed regulatory restriction. The granddaddy of all regulatory restrictions, though, is the U.S. Government. When Uncle Sam isn't writing down explicit regulations in the form of legislation such as the Sarbanes-Oxley Act, he has a collection of agencies busy creating and revising regulations that have very tangible effects upon our daily business life. The IRS, SEC, and Employment Standards Administration are probably most notable in this respect. Just because the regulatory noose doesn't appear on your radar, though, does not mean that it is not a threat. You may be saying to yourselves "I don't have to worry about Sarbanes-Oxley" and other publicly traded company restrictions, but I wouldn't rest well at night with that thinking. All it takes is one thorough audit of one of your publicly-traded clients to realize that non-compliant service suppliers are the weak link in their certification chain. Then the edict will come to comply or be gone. Your competitors may react more quickly and provide your client with an easy decision in regards to preferred service provider.

What if you were to "out do" the global business process outsourcers? In keeping with the old adage that the best defense is a good offense, turn your bricks-and-mortar business into a bricks-and-clicks e-business. Bricks and mortar refers to traditional business models that feature little or no internet presence. Bricks and clicks refers to innovative business models that leverage the full capabilities of the internet to expand their footprint globally. The latter strategy is most successful if the internet presence is simply a controlled extension of its internal business processes. This approach requires a process-based business culture which can be challenging for free-spirited entrepreneurs. If given a competitive choice, most U.S. businesses still prefer the good ol' Made in USA label.

What if you were able to go beyond documenting your procedures for complying with regulatory guidance and actually provided auditors with data that confirms your compliance? While document management systems such as SharePoint allow you to post your policies centrally for all employees to see, business process management systems such as AgilePoint provide you with the ability to track the execution of procedures established to enforce those policies. The best way to tackle audits is proactively.

Step 1 Review

As we can see, this strange new world of IT offers some intriguing benefits for Professional Service Firms daring enough to venture into its borders. Our SWOT analysis summarized in **Table 2** provided us with some insights into where most Professional Service Firms are before they start cruising on the information super-highway.

Table 2 / SWOT Analysis

Strengths	Weaknesses	Opportunities	Threats
· Domain knowledge · Low overhead · Portability of business model · Client Relationships · Simplicity · Reputation	· Lack of IT expertise · Limited geographic reach · Significant variation in business practices from employee to employee · Sensititivity to employee turnover	· Market expansion · Increased responsiveness · Improved expectation management · Delivery quality · Improved knowledge sharing · More efficient delivery of high-volume, low-margin accounts · Lower administrative burden	· Outsourced business processes · Regulations

This SWOT analysis is deliberately high-level and is designed to help you shape your business strategy. If you were to hand this assessment off to an IT vendor and say "give me an IT product that leverages my strengths, mitigates my weaknesses, takes advantages of my opportunities, and diminishes my threats", chances are that you would shortly find yourself either broke or very disappointed. We need to fill the communication gap with IT vendors with a bit more bridgework. This means that we need to define our business in more detail in order to effectively marry the information of your business to the appropriate technology suitor. In order to measure and improve the movement of information, we need to "look under the hood" of your business operations to see exactly what these parcels of information are and how they interact with one another.

You have now passed by the following IT Roadmap milestone:

Step 1 | **Business SIPOC Model** | **SWOT Analysis**

STEP 2: HOW DO YOU DO IT?

"For want of a nail...
a shoe was lost.
For want of a shoe...
the horse was lost.
For want of a horse...
the rider was lost.
For want of a rider...
the battle was lost."

Anonymous

Where are the nails in your business operations? I recall early in my career that a single bolt held up the shipment of a $700,000 system. Through late shipment penalties and strained relations with our customer, this little bolt provided us with a fairly tangible measure of the cost of poor information. For you, it may not be information about the location of a nail or a bolt. Perhaps it is information about the status of an invoice or who is available to best provide services to your new client. In the case of our little bolt, the crucial information about its location was hidden with the bolt somewhere in the confines of our shop. Do you have any information like that in your business? Your bolts may not be hidden amidst the vastness of a manufacturing shop floor. Maybe you face the daunting task of extracting the information from the walking, talking hard drives of your business – your people. While knowing where a morsel of information can be found is a very practical piece of information during the course of the business day, there is another, more practical, question for businesses considering the pursuit of information technology. How did the information get there? Another way of saying this is "How do you do what you do?" More to the point, how would you communicate to someone else (say, an IT vendor) what you do? Chances are that you would start your description off with many of the keywords cited in the high-level business model shown in **Figure 5.** This level of information might suffice for casual dinner conversation, but it still leaves a lot to the imagination for folks interested in helping you do what you do better. Room for imagination equates to room for significant financial risk when it comes to deploying IT solutions. Before you deploy information technology for your business, it will be much easier if you have a solid understanding of not only where the nails are in your business, but also how they got there. In this section, we will be laying the groundwork for you to answer both of these questions for your business.

Organization

In order to find and track your business nails, we first need to clean up shop and get organized. Growing up in the Motor City, I am heavily influenced by the trends and technology of the manufacturing industry even though I no longer work in it. What does manufacturing have to do with Professional Service Firms you say? Quite a bit as it turns out. But first, let's take a look at how they are different. The principle assets in Professional Service Firms are people, while in manufacturing companies it is fair to say it is the equipment that blankets the factory floor. This manufacturing equipment is technology specifically designed to help people to do their job more effectively. Once Professional Service Firms decide to employ technology to help them do their job more effectively, they have crossed into a realm that begs an examination of what can be learned from the manufacturing industry.

Technology, even information technology, tends to have quite a limited intellect. What I mean is that if your attempts to communicate with a given technology are not structured in a language that it knows, you will have quite a bit of difficulty getting it to perform the task in a manner to your liking. Modern manufacturing plants are huge capital investments involving hundreds of millions of dollars. The last thing you want after investing all of that money is to have a collection of machinery that doesn't communicate well with your workforce. In order to make cost-effective use of these investments and the labor force that makes them work, the manufacturing industry has developed what are arguably some of the most progressive methods for business performance improvement.

One of the nuggets found in the manufacturing industry is the concept of the 5S System. The 5S System is a set of activities that set the stage for business performance improvement. These activities are as follows:

- Sort
- Set in Order
- Shine
- Standardize
- Sustain

We will be addressing all of these activities in this section in one form or another, but I would like to focus on the **Set in Order** activity for our discussion on organization. The **"Set in Order"** activity is simply another way of saying "get organized".
Why is it important to get organized?

How much time and money does your organization lose trying to find information? Some of the following questions may sound familiar:

- Who is responsible for approving this expense report?
- What assets can we depreciate on our tax returns?
- How much are we spending on telephone services?
- Where can I find all of the who's, what's, and how's of our organization?

You need to be able to find "things" before you can improve them. If you can't find these nuggets of information, how are you going to tell a computer where to find them?

Value of Organization

If you align the structure of your resources to the structure of your finances then in turn to the structure of your data, it will be much easier to deploy most advanced IT solutions. It will be easier to identify the people responsible for specific data or financial performance. It also will be easier to identify how financial performance objectives affect your resources, and it will be easier to establish a security model to control who gets to see what data.

The quest to get organized starts with the following areas:

- Resources (People, Technology, Services)
- Finances
- Data

Just like a child depends upon healthy bones to grow into a healthy adult, your business needs a solid structural foundation for your resources, finances, and business data. Take advantage of the fact that you are a small business with relatively simple and pliant structures that will grow with you rather than work against you, as is the case with many larger corporations.

RESOURCES

A day in the life of your business features the movement of a lot of information. This information does not move itself. Someone or something has to give it a push. We will refer to this "someone" or "something" as a "resource". Resources are assets that need to be managed effectively to keep information flowing smoothly throughout your business. As you continue to consider the IT Roadmap that your organization will follow, you will increasingly face the question as to whether or not your performance targets could be met most effectively with more employees, better technology or an external service provider. In order to set ourselves up for apples-to-apples-to-apples comparisons of what may appear at first glance to be apples-to-oranges-to-kumquats comparisons, we need to get these assets organized.

PEOPLE

The first thing that people think of when they hear the term "organization" in a business sense is an "org chart". This is how people are "Set in Order". Many companies do not even have organization charts. Organizations charts can change so often in some businesses that it doesn't seem worth the time required to put one on paper. If you want to know who's responsible for doing what, you just pick up the phone or holler across the cubicle and ask the person who seems to be plugged in to the latest thinking of senior management. Computers, though, are different than people. They tend to spend less time at the water cooler and, as a result, are typically clueless as to who really knows what is going on inside the office. If they need to know who's in charge of approving expense reports, they need to be explicitly told who the person is.

Now, you typically won't find any software code that says "Jane approves expense reports". Software code is typically organized by functions, not people, and this code is often organized by functions at quite a granular level. During the installation of advanced software packages, the permission to use each of the functions in the software is defined by what IT providers call a "security model". Security models featuring groups of individuals organized by functional responsibilities are much easier to set up and manage afterwards than security models defined at the individual level. New users can be assigned to groups already associated with standard functional permissions ▶

Figure 6 Basic Functional Organizations

rather than needing to be configured individually. Could you define your security models on the basis of individual names? - Yes.
Is it recommended? - No.

Since this book is geared towards helping you communicate better with the world of IT, it would be helpful if you were to define your core organization chart on the basis of functions rather than people. The basic functions within a typical Professional Services Firm are depicted in **Figure 6.** These functions will be the manufacturing equivalent of color-coded bins to help with our 5S methodology. Now we need to figure out how to connect our people to these functional bins.

Most small businesses start out with a single person (usually the owner) responsible for managing all of these bins. As the business grows, the owner will most likely need to divide up the functional responsibilities between members of the growing organization. A popular approach to these responsibilities in a Professional Service Firm is to divide them into staff and support organizations. The staff organization is typically assigned sales, marketing and service delivery responsibilities, while the support organization takes care of the rest. **Figure 7** provides one example of the evolutionary path that the management responsibilities in a Professional Services Firm may take as it grows. The key point of this figure is that while the faces may change, the core functions in the business do not.

Figure 7 Connecting Functions to People

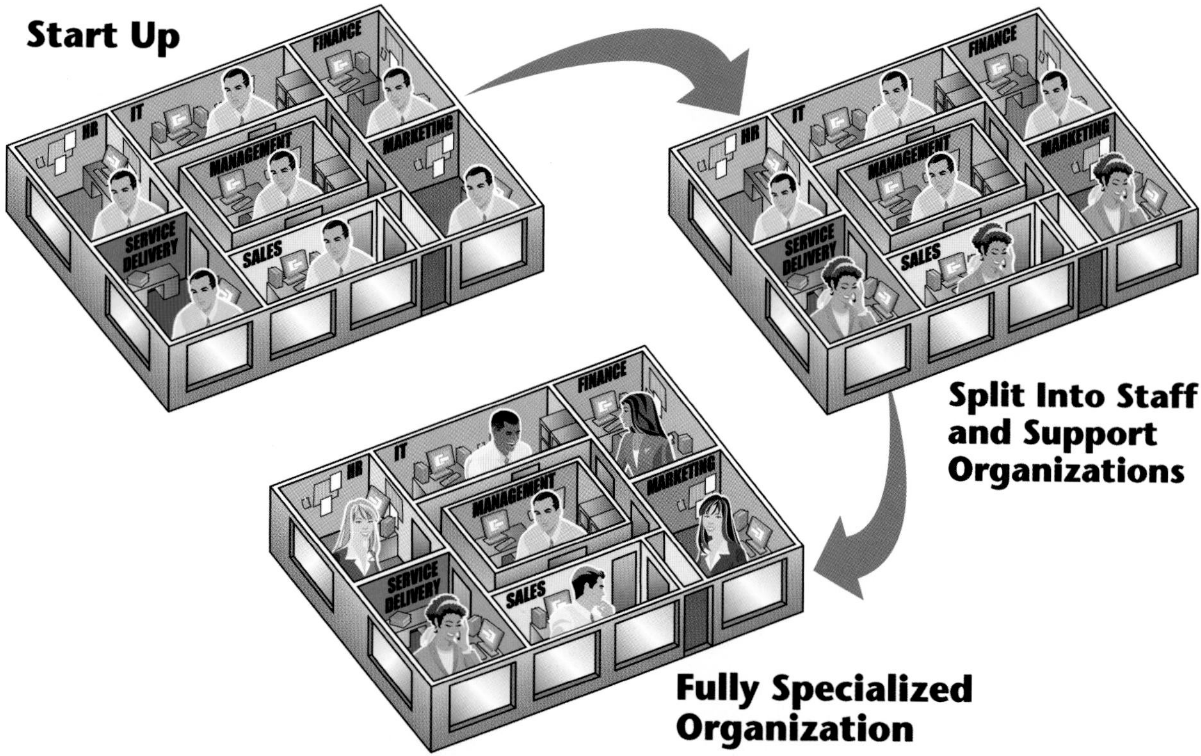

While service offerings and personnel may change quite a bit over time, the basic functions do not change much. Save yourself the pain of re-organizations – start with a function-based organization chart. Like the positions on a sports team, the names of the positions in your business don't change, only the names of the players that play those positions change. To do anything else would require rewriting the playbook that we will draw up later in this section. If we rewrite the playbook after we have already trained a team of dimwitted software programs how to execute the plays in accordance with the various positions, your team will have a poor performance at the big game. Throughout the remainder of this book, our discussions will assume that you have a fully specialized organization. If this is not how you have organized your people, remember that you will have the opportunity to build your own personal IT Roadmap tuned to your operations.

TECHNOLOGY

Do you have a consolidated list of all of your computers and software programs? Do you know which software programs have been installed on which computers? Do you know which employee uses which computer? The answers to these questions are often a simple "no". Important reasons exist as to why you should do your best to answer "yes" to these questions. Some of the most straightforward reasons include the fact that copying software without sufficient license coverage is illegal and the fact that the cost of software and hardware has tax implications. However, the reason most pertinent to this book is that "yes" answers will help you to evaluate the business benefit of your IT strategy.

Software

Software can be expensive. As with most expensive purchases, it is important to keep track of where and how it is being used. While software can be purchased in a box like other office supplies, it differs from its shrink-wrapped brethren in that it can be readily copied. Software companies devote significant research and development funds to creating these products. These companies recoup their investments by charging customers for the privilege of copying their software to their hardware devices, otherwise known as licensing.

Software licensing can be quite complicated. A quick introduction to the different licensing options for software is provided in **Table 3**. The license landscape is further complicated by "Software Assurance Programs" which ensure regular updates of your software suite provided you keep up to date on your "premiums".

Table 3 / Software License Types

License Type	Description	Advantages	Disadvantages
User (aka Client Access License or CAL)	Provides license to use software on an individual user basis.	Software can be installed on multiple devices so long as it services the same user account. Users can have access to their software from any device on the network.	If there are more employees than devices, it may not be economical.
Device (aka computer)	Provides license to use software on an individual device basis.	Software can support multiple users on a single device.	If employees use more than one device, it may not be economical (e.g. laptop and desktop).
Site	Provides license for unlimited usage of software for a specific company or site within a company.	Mitigates the need to track installation of software by user or device. Simplifies the procurement cycle for licenses.	Can be very expensive.
Concurrent Users	Provides license for a certain number of simultaneous user sessions.	Often less expensive than purchasing licenses for all users or devices in an organization.	Only suitable for server-based applications. May result in application access denial during peak usage periods.
Demo	Provides license to use software for a specified trial period.	Useful for evaluating software prior to purchasing.	Access to software will expire. Often not full featured.

Despite the complexities that sometimes arise with software licensing, if your business is properly organized, you should not draw a bead of sweat if someone were to audit the copies of software that you have made against the licenses that you have for that software. Get your software bin neat and tidy. **Table 4** offers one example of a worksheet that could be used to track software usage and licensing compliance for your business.

Table 4 / Sample License Tracking Worksheet

Software	Device or User	Version	Vendor	License Type	# Instances	
					Allowed	Actual
Office Professional		2003	Microsoft	Device	2	2
	Laptop-001					*1*
	Laptop-002					*1*
Windows		XP	Microsoft	Device	2	2
	Laptop-001					*1*
	Laptop-002					*1*
Virtual PC		2004	Microsoft	Device	1	1
	Laptop-001					*1*
Small Business Server		2003	Microsoft	CAL	5	2
	Steve Sales					*1*
	Fran Finance					*1*

Hardware

Software is no good unless you have hardware on which to install it and from which you can operate it. It is very rare in Professional Services Firms nowadays to have an employee without a computer of his or her own (known as a "dedicated" computer). Often, employees have more than one computer – perhaps a desktop PC for the office and a laptop for the road. Employees often have these assets supplemented by personal digital assistants (PDAs) and smart phones that need to be kept synchronized with their other hardware. A host of other "peripherals" will add to the cornucopia of computer equipment found in the typical office. Printers, displays, and scanners are some of the most obvious, but there are many other devices typically required to keep your computer-based operations running smoothly. These devices include routers, hubs, modems, and servers, most of which tends to be quite expensive.

Keeping track of your hardware assets can be important not only from a licensing perspective, but also come tax time. **Table 5** represents one way of tracking your hardware assets.

Table 5 / Sample Hardware Worksheet

Hardware	Assigned To	Functional Department	Software	Version	Vendor	License Type	# Instances	
							Allowed	**Actual**
Laptop-001	Steve Sales	Sales	*Windows*	*XP*	*Microsoft*	*Device*	*1*	*1*
			Office Professional	*2003*	*Microsoft*	*Device*	*1*	*1*
Laptop-002	Fran Finance	Finance	*Windows*	*XP*	*Microsoft*	*Device*	*1*	*1*
			Office Professional	*2003*	*Microsoft*	*Device*	*1*	*1*
Server-001	NA	IT	*Small Business Server*	*2003*	*Microsoft*	*CAL*	*5*	*2*
Printer-001	NA	IT	*NA*	*NA*	*NA*	*NA*	*NA*	*NA*

Architecture

In order to share information between software applications or between different hardware devices, we need to make some connections. The diagram depicting these connections is often called an Architecture diagram. Architecture[1] is defined by the American Heritage Dictionary as the "orderly arrangement of parts; structure". Most businesses have many moving parts that need to be arranged in an orderly manner. In regards to software and hardware, these arrangements are often depicted as software and hardware architecture diagrams. If you standardize your organization on a single software platform, it will not be necessary to worry about your software architecture, but you will want to get your arms around your hardware or "physical" architecture.

Before we delve into defining a typical physical architecture for a Professional Services Firm, we should probably go over some networking basics. Networks convert individual (standalone) computers and software applications into systems that share information. Businesses are most effective when information is shared (within regulatory restrictions). In the same way that people share information with other people by "networking", computers also share information via networks. The basic types of computer networking approaches most commonly found are depicted in **Figure 8** and summarized below:

- **Sneakernet:** No physical or wireless connections between computers. Files are transferred via floppy disks, CD-ROM, flash drives or the like.
- **Peer-to-peer:** Computers are connected via cables or wirelessly. Connections often include the use of a hub or router.
- **Client-Server:** Client-Server network with internet access is the current model for an advanced network. A server is similar in many ways to your desktop PC. In fact, many desktop PC's can be used as servers for some organizations. The primary difference is the purpose of the device. Servers provide centralized "services" to your users. A typical use of a server is security (i.e. who can access what data), but there are many specialized server options such as web servers, database servers, print servers, and file servers. Unlike the other types of networks, servers in a client-server network typically run around the clock.

[1] *The American Heritage® Dictionary of the English Language, Fourth Edition*

Figure 8 Types of Networks

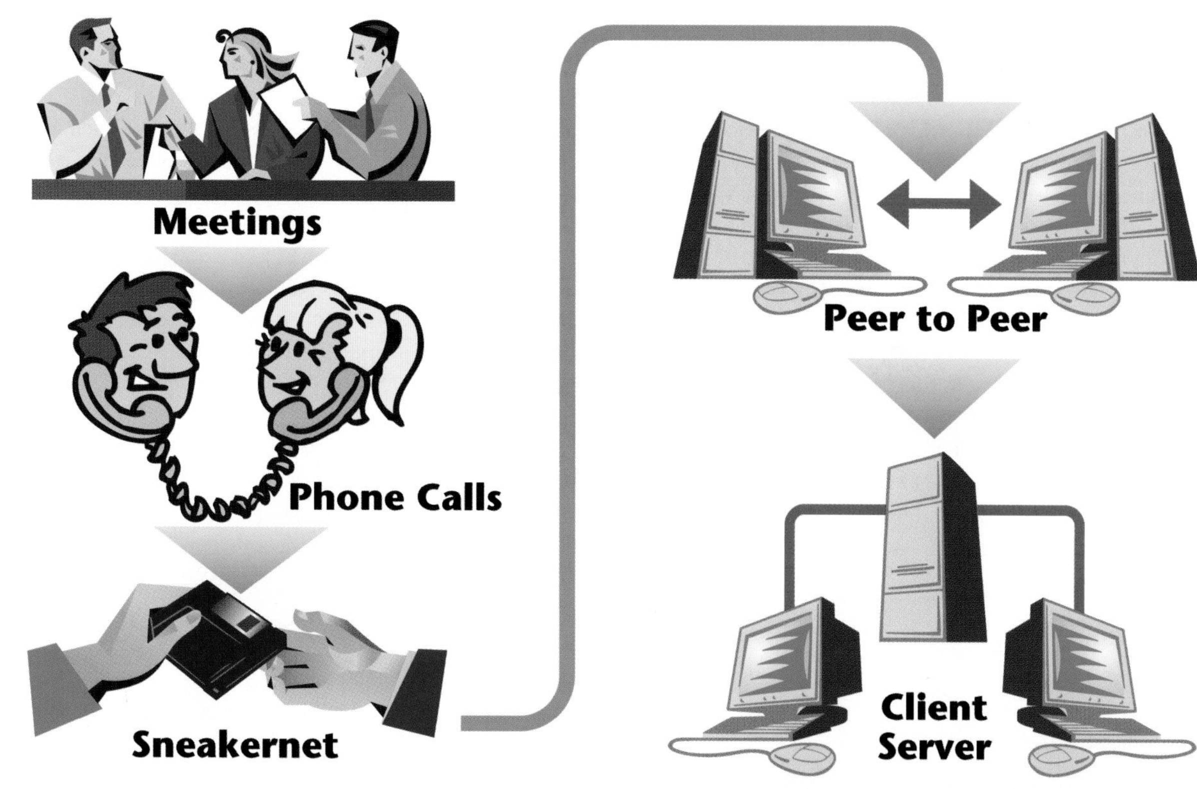

In addition to the various "types" of networks available, networks can also vary in scope as depicted in **Figure 9.** The scope pertains to the types of people that can access information on your network. The following network scopes are typically found:

- **Intranet:** The scope of access is typically limited to personnel within the confines of your office building. This network is often referred to as a Local Area Network or LAN.
- **Extranet:** The scope of access is extended to remote users with the proper security credentials to access your company intranet or subset thereof using the public internet. A common secure-access method for users is a Virtual Private Network or VPN connection.
- **Internet:** The scope of this access is literally the world. This type of network connection features unsecured, general access to company information that you choose to host outside of your company firewall (e.g. your website). The internet is the most extreme example of what is sometimes referred to as a Wide Area Network or WAN.

A detailed physical architecture diagram for a Professional Services Firm might look something like that depicted in **Figure 10.** The majority of the movement of information occurs on the company intranet behind a security device called a firewall. Firewalls can be implemented via software or via hardware devices. Employees at remote sites such as client sites or at home are able to access the company intranet through a secure connection resulting in the formation of an extranet. Internet surfers from around the world are able to access a web server via an internet connection.

Figure 9 Network Scope

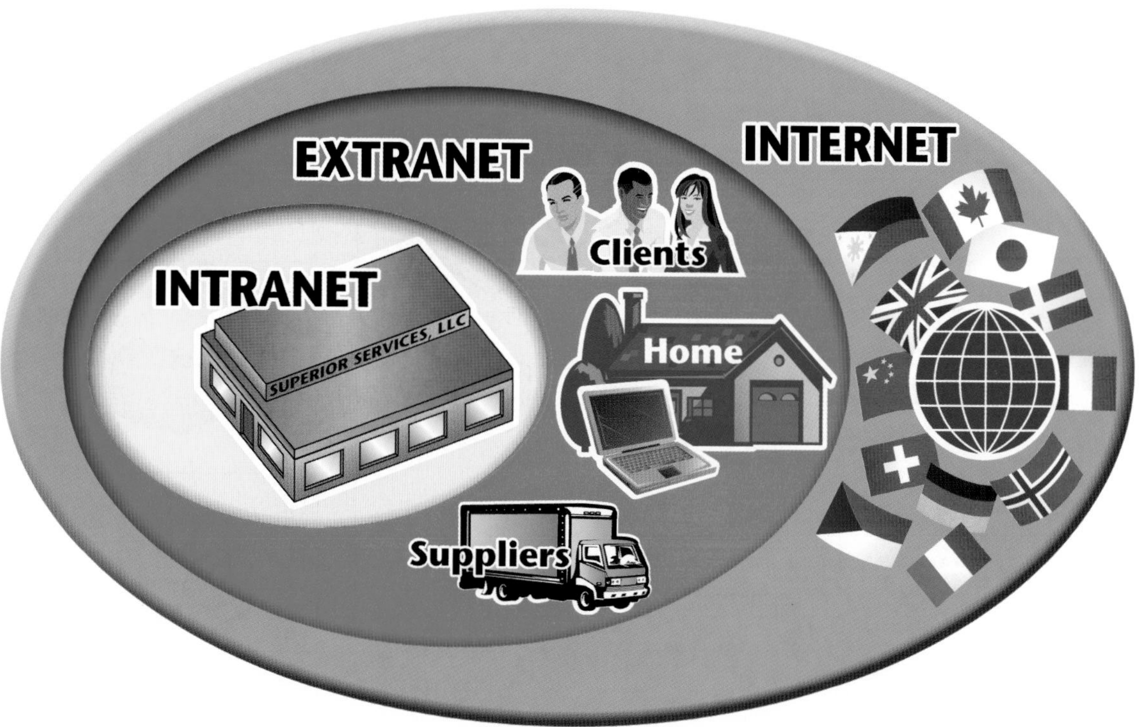

Figure 10 Sample Physical Architecture

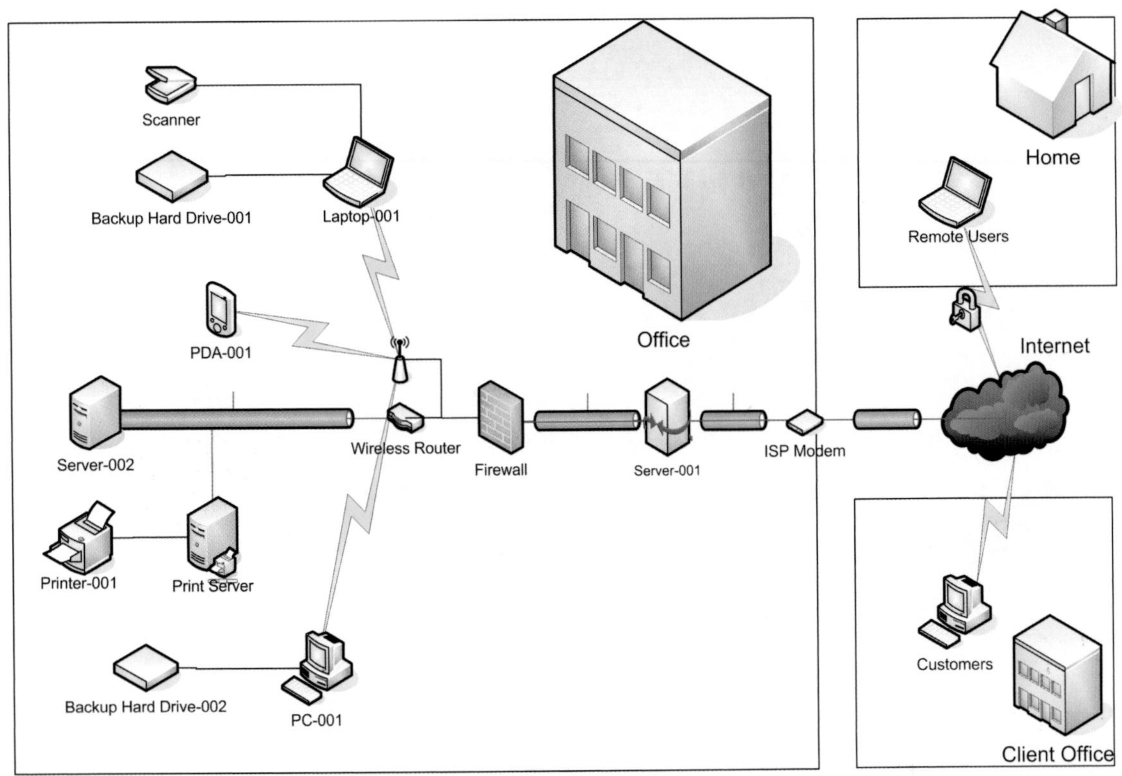

SERVICES

Does all this technology jargon sound a bit overwhelming? Have no fear. A variety of service providers are in business to help lighten the load. These service companies are resources as well. Chances are that your company uses service companies to support multiple aspects of your business, but let's focus on the following technology-related services:

- **Internet Service Provider (ISP):** Provides your company with access to the internet.
- **Managed Service Provider:** Provides infrastructure services such as website hosting, data recovery and backup, and remote system support.
- **Application Service Provider (ASP):** Provides "Software as a Service". Rather than pay what can often be a substantial upfront cost for software licenses, companies can "lease" licenses to software over the internet in a "pay as you go" manner.

In order to avoid billing surprises that could adversely impact your cash flow, it is important to "set these resources in order" as you have done with your personnel and technology. Be sure that you have a clear understanding of the following information pertaining to these resources:

- Who is responsible for the oversight of the Service Level Agreement (SLA)?
- What are the cost drivers for these services (e.g. duration of calls, storage space)?
- What information is transferred between organizations and how is this performed?

Your suppliers are an extension of your business. They allow you to focus on the core functions of your business. Just remember that while you might be able to outsource these functions, you cannot outsource the impact of these organizations upon the performance of your business.

FINANCES

The Chart of Accounts is your key to getting your business in order. Depending upon how the Chart of Accounts has been set up, finding the right account, or set thereof, can be like a game of financial roulette. You spin through the list of accounts a few times until it settles into a space on the wheel. To make matters worse, the next time you take a spin on the wheel with the same information, you find yourself landing on another space. It is a marvel that there are not more Enron's in industry.

The types of accounts typically found in a Chart of Accounts for a Professional Services Firm are as follows:

- Asset accounts
- Liability accounts
- Revenue accounts
- Expense accounts

The cost of assets such as software and hardware fit neatly into your asset accounts. The loans that you may take out to pay for these assets may fit nicely into the liability accounts. The entries for the revenue and expense accounts will be covered in **Step 3,** but the structure of these accounts is worth addressing now.

Often, the Chart of Accounts is defined in a vacuum by a finance department struggling to satisfy the voracious needs of government tax forms **(See Table 6).**

This approach is often detrimental to the needs of folks who have simple questions, such as "how much does it cost to run my HR department?" Significant information-management benefits can arise from a more collaborative approach to defining the Chart of Accounts. As the gateway to key decisions, a well-crafted Chart of Accounts will help you make effective, consistent decisions. Since most of these decisions are driven by financial information, it is critical that each business function has the information it needs to make its decisions while still satisfying the reporting needs of Uncle Sam.

How can we create a Chart of Accounts that sets the stage for the improvement of our business performance? I recommend the following guidelines wherever practical:

- Leverage multi-tier account structure wherever practical. Upper tiers should be simple and not subject to change.
- Lower tiers should feature entries that may be volatile from year to year (e.g. tax line items).
- Create explicit entries for the ▶

Table 6 / Chart of Accounts

Account	Name	Type
1000	Petty Cash	Cash Account
1010	Checking	Bank
1100	Savings	Bank
1200	Accounts Receivable	Accounts Receivable
1230	Deposits	Other Current Asset
1240	Federal Income Tax	Other Current Asset
1420	Office Equipment	Fixed Asset
1430	Professional Equip	Fixed Asset
1460	Accumulated depreciation	Fixed Asset
2000	Accounts Payable	Accounts Payable
2100	Credit Card	Current Liability
2200	Payroll Liabilities	Current Liability
2205	P/R Liab-FWH;S/S; Medicare	Current Liability
2215	P/R Liab- State, Local	Current Liability
2225	P/R Liab-401K	Current Liability
2230	P/R Liab-Profit Sharing	Current Liability
2235	P/R Liab-Medical & Dental	Current Liability
2240	P/R Liab-Section 125	Current Liability
2310	Salaries Accrued-FYE	Current Liability
2330	Federal Income Tax Payable	Current Liability
2400	Shareholder/Stockholder Loan	Current Liability
5010	Billable Time	Cost of Goods Sold
5015	Outside Consultants (Billable)	Cost of Goods Sold
5140	Outsourced Labor	Cost of Goods Sold
8191	Reseller Software	Cost of Goods Sold
6010	Advertising & Promotion	Expense
6015	Marketing/Printed Materials	Expense
6020	Website	Expense
6025	Amortization	Expense
6070	Contract Labor	Expense
6080	Contributions/Donations	Expense
6090	Depreciation	Expense
7510	Telecommunications	Expense
7710	Travel	Expense
7810	Utilities	Expense

accounts in your business: customers, suppliers, functional organizations.

- Explicitly list each of your service offerings.
- If possible, assign a unique account to each activity in context of its parent functional organization.
- Ensure that all tax fields are explicitly listed as individual lines in context of the form supported by the entry.
- Ensure that you will be capable of operating each functional organization as a profit-and-loss center and not simply a cost center.

Ideally, each journal entry could be associated with multiple classification fields with each classification field satisfying a different user audience. Due to the need for historical traceability and the observation that multi-tier account structures are not practical without computers, this capability is not being pushed hard in industry. There are signs of change on the horizon, though. Vendors are starting to offer multi-dimensional financial data tracking software. Due to the enhanced data-mining capabilities that these solutions will offer your business, it would be wise to prepare for the usage of this software and think multi-tier when defining your Chart of Accounts.

Remember the roulette wheel scenario – your financial reports are only as good as the data entry. It is crucial that the classification of your financial data during entry is intuitive and repeatable. Your financial data is arguably the most important set of information that you collect, but your Chart of Accounts will be filled with negative signs in the wrong places if you do not keep tabs on the commerce of other information within your business.

DATA

How would you find a book in a library without the Dewey Decimel System? How would you expect to find information in your business without similar structures? If you want to know which person to go to, refer to the org chart. If you want to know where your money is being spent, you refer to the Chart of Accounts. Where do you go to find the rest of the information in your business?

Let's introduce a new organizing structure into your business: the information model. The information model is the Information Age equivalent of color-coded folders in a file cabinet. Information is organized into logical sets of data, starting with your business as a whole. Within your business you have two primary classes of information. You have information pertaining to your current business operations on one hand. On the other hand, you have information pertaining to your attempts to change the performance of these operations. The former corresponds to process data; the latter corresponds to project data. Processes are essential elements of your daily operations, while projects are typically discretionary. This is an important distinction when it comes to making decisions about how to allocate limited funds throughout your business. If you are in a budget crunch, are you more likely to eliminate the HR function or cancel a project to renovate your office building?

The information model defined in **Figure 11** represents the recommended Dewey Decimel System for your business information. This information may start out as organized into file cabinets but as you improve your IT infrastructure you will be able to replicate this structure with your computer system. Once you have this information organized and stored on your network, you will be able to find it more easily, share it more easily and put it to better use than ever before. We now have our resources (people, technology and services), finances and our data in order. Now let's take a look at how the information in your business is put to use today.

Figure 11 Business Information Model

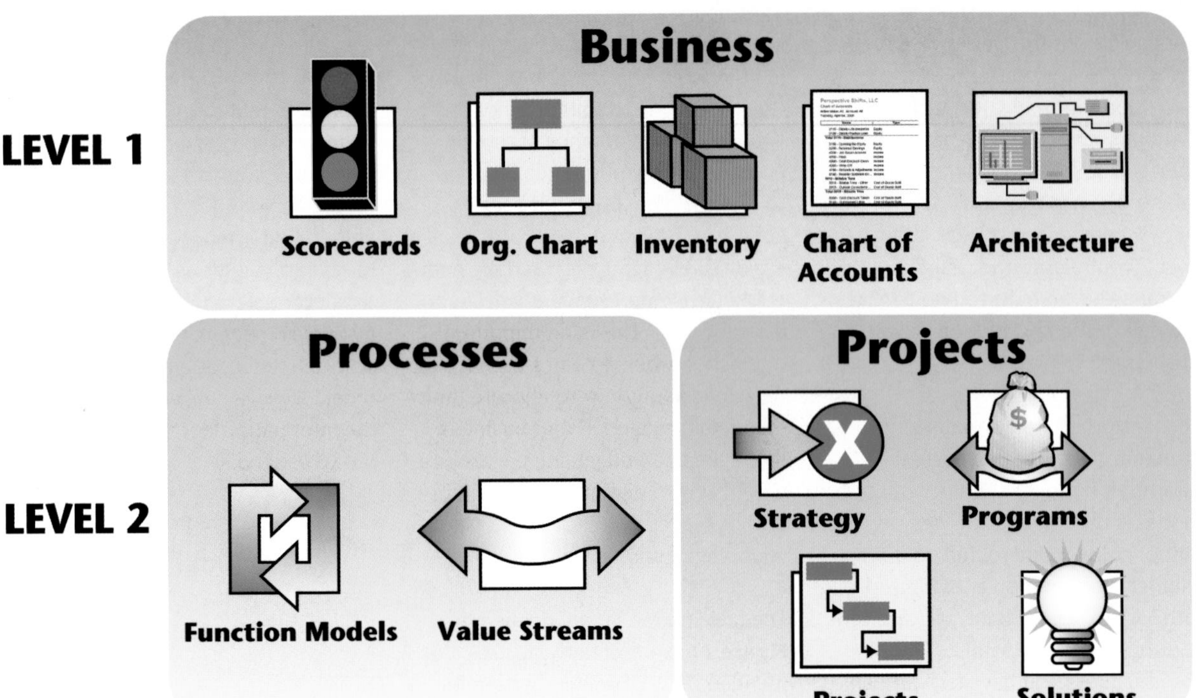

Process Models

A lot goes on inside of the functional bins originally defined in **Figure 6** that is relevant to implementing information technology. In this section, we will not only look at what information moves between organizations, we will also look under the hood of each organization to see what makes it run.

Processes persist while technology turns over.

An inherently high degree of interdependency exists between functional organizations, yet in most businesses they operate as if they were independent, not dependent. If you are a sole proprietor without any employees, you should not have this problem unless you have other problems beyond the scope of this book. If you have reached a point in your business where you do have employees, the following circumstances may seem familiar:

- Sales landed a contract for immediate support but no one is available to deliver it.
- HR has hired a new employee, but IT has no computer for them.
- Marketing generated several leads from an event, but Sales did not know of them in time to follow-up on any of them.
- The delivery team completed their engagement in less time than estimated, yet Finance billed the client as if they provided the estimated billable time.

Stovepipes

One of the undesirable side effects of dividing your people into functional organizations is the creation of information "stovepipes". The impractical alternative to this approach is for everyone to become experts in all aspects of running the business. Information technology provides the means of connecting these stovepipes together without sacrificing the productivity advantages associated with allowing personnel to focus on a specific function.

What is the common ingredient in these circumstances? For whatever reason, the information in one person's cranium did not make it to the cranium of someone else in the organization. The failure to provide this information in a timely manner resulted in the loss of time – which translates either to unnecessary expenses or lost revenue opportunities. In order to avoid these failures, we need to gain a better understanding of how each organization does its job. We will be packaging this understanding within process models.

Software is simply a process translated into a language or protocol that a computer understands. In order for software to be able to help you, you need to speak its language or get someone to translate for you. Software involves moving discrete packets of information from point A to point B. Process models do not need to be detailed in order to be useful in describing this movement of information. As your business becomes more comfortable with process modeling, you can add more detail. For now, let's simply get the ball rolling. For simplicity, we'll assume a fully specialized functional organization in accordance with **Figure 7.** The manager for each functional department is responsible for all of the tasks within the functional process model for their organization. They may not perform all of the tasks within the process, but they are responsible for the performance of the tasks. To model a typical "day in the life", we will follow along in the tasks of a fictitious professional firm, Superior Services, and its personnel:

- Steve our Sales Manager
- Mary our Marketing Manager
- Debra our Service Delivery Manager
- Helen our Human Resources Manager

Tasks

Tasks are the basic building blocks of Service Oriented Architectures (SOA). In a nutshell, SOA departs from earlier software architecture concepts by seeking to break up large, fairly inflexible software programs into bite-size chunks. Web-based delivery is a fundamental aspect of most SOA-based programs.

- Fran our Finance Manager
- Ian our IT Manager
- Mike our General Manager

Ultimately, you will need to assign your personnel to functional responsibilities and define the process models in a manner that describes how you do business. These process models of Superior Services have been defined to provide a common reference. They are deliberately basic and perhaps even a bit ideal, but they should be a good starting point for most businesses that have yet to define how they do what they do. Now, by way of Superior Services, let's take a deeper look into how many Professional Service Firms operate. If you define how you do what you do in a manner similar to the next sections you will have a core understanding of your business that you can use to clearly convey your business needs to IT solution providers.

Standard Processes

Having a set of standard processes that describe your business operations not only satisfies the "Standardize" element of the 5S methodology, it also sets the stage for the following activities:

- New employee orientation
- Training
- Auditing (banks, investors, government)
- Expectation management with IT vendors

SALES

The primary responsibility of Steve our Sales Manager is the conversion of sales leads to contracts. His performance is often measured in terms of sales revenue and closure rate for the leads with which he has been provided. In order to perform his job well, Steve relies upon information from his customers, Marketing, IT, partners, and the Service Delivery team. This information can be summarized as follows:

- Leads
- Contracts
- Marketing Materials
- Case Studies

The information packets provided by the Steve's Sales organization are as follows:

- Proposals
- Sales Orders, Contract Confirmations or Statements of Work

- Client References
- Customer Needs

The flow of information coming into and out of Steve's area is summarized in **Figure 12.** **Figure 13** reflects a look under the hood at the processes specific to Sales. The same approach will be taken to provide a high-level description of the processes specific to other functional organizations within the business as described in **Figure 6.**

Figure 12 Sales SIPOC Model

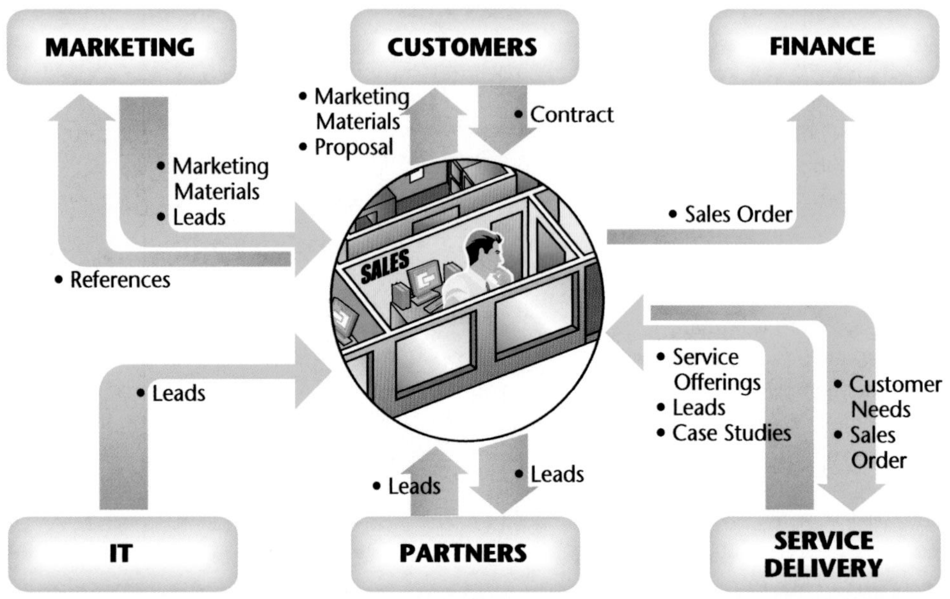

Steve our Sales Manager starts his day by booting up his computer and reviewing an assortment of emails that he has received. Several of these emails contain potential sales leads that he'll need to follow up on. When he checks his voice mail, he finds a few messages that indicate even more potential sales leads. He adds these leads to the list from yesterday. Luckily, business has been good. It has been so good Steve needs to prioritize which leads he will address first. After jotting down a few notes about which leads warrant immediate attention, he calls up the source of each lead to find out more information, such as what services are required and when. The investigation and follow-up for these leads takes the better portion of the day, leaving little time to follow-up with current clients.

Some of the services required by prospective clients go beyond the current list of service offerings for the firm, so Steve asks Debra in Delivery to evaluate how they might approach providing these services in a new offering. Some of the leads are simply requests for more information about current service offerings. These requests for information are easily satisfied by a package dropped in the mail featuring a cover letter and a few copies of existing marketing materials. Steve sets out to develop proposals for leads that indicate an immediate need for services. Sometimes the proposal is as simple as calling the prospective client and conveying the firm's hourly rate, but sometimes the proposal requires a more systematic approach. Steve logs which of the proposals have been accepted and promptly calls Debra in Delivery to get a Service Delivery specialist assigned to customers that have approved of proposals.

It turns out that today is Friday. Every Friday, Steve is required to submit a status report for Sales to Mike in Management. Revenue is up so far this quarter, but Steve feels overwhelmed by the sheer volume of leads and the amount of time and effort it takes to investigate each of them.

If we were to diagram this typical day in the life of Steve our Sales Manager, it might look something like the process model shown in **Figure 13.** This model amounts to the basic playbook for the Sales organization.

Figure 13 Sales Process Model

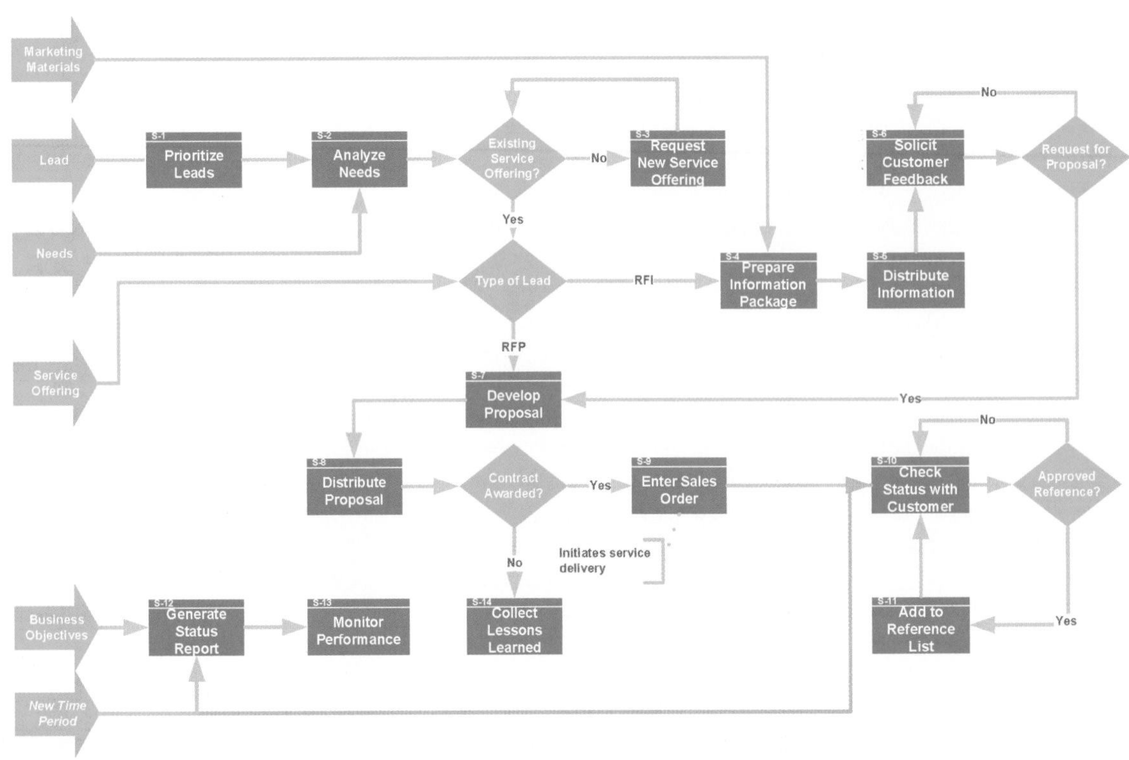

MARKETING

The primary responsibility of Mary our Marketing Manager is the generation of sales leads. Her performance is often measured in terms of the number and quality of sales leads generated through her marketing efforts. In order to perform her job well, Mary relies upon information from her customers, Sales, and the Service Delivery team. This information can be summarized as follows:

- Leads
- Contracts
- Marketing Materials
- Case Studies

The information packets provided by the Marketing organization are as follows:

- Leads
- Marketing Materials
- Customer Needs

The flow of information coming into and out of the Marketing organization is summarized in **Figure 14.** Mary our Marketing Manager starts off her day in much the same manner as Steve. She boots up her computer, gets a cup of coffee, and delves into a stream of emails that she has received since leaving the office yesterday. Nothing demands her immediate attention, but a few events cited in her daily market blogs warrant attention. She marks up the calendar on her wall with the dates for the events. Two of the events require arranging for a booth to support their standard exhibit display. She sends a quick note to Ian in IT to add a banner to the website promoting their attendance at the event. Mary has been analyzing ways to take advantage of their internet presence to increase the number of qualified leads for Sales, but it appears that plenty of leads are in the sales pipeline for the time being. Later in the day, she hears rumors of a new service offering being developed and makes a note to notify her staff to work with the Service Delivery team to create some marketing materials around the new offering. Before she leaves the office, she ▶

CRM

Customer Relationship Management (CRM) software provides sales and marketing organizations with the ability to generate and track communications with customers and prospects. Samples of CRM solutions are profiled in the appendix of this book.

pulls together her Friday status report for Mike. In her report, she emphasizes that the market is ripe for their services, but they have failed to scale the organization effectively to meet the demand.

If we were to diagram a typical day in the life of Mary our Marketing Manager, it might look something like that shown in **Figure 15.**

Figure 14 Marketing SIPOC Model

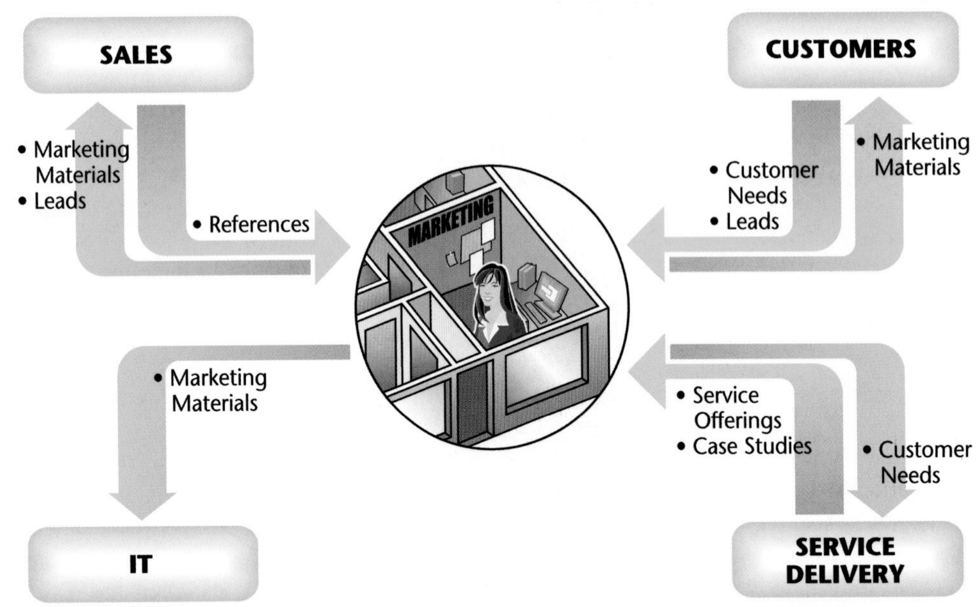

Figure 15 Marketing Process Model

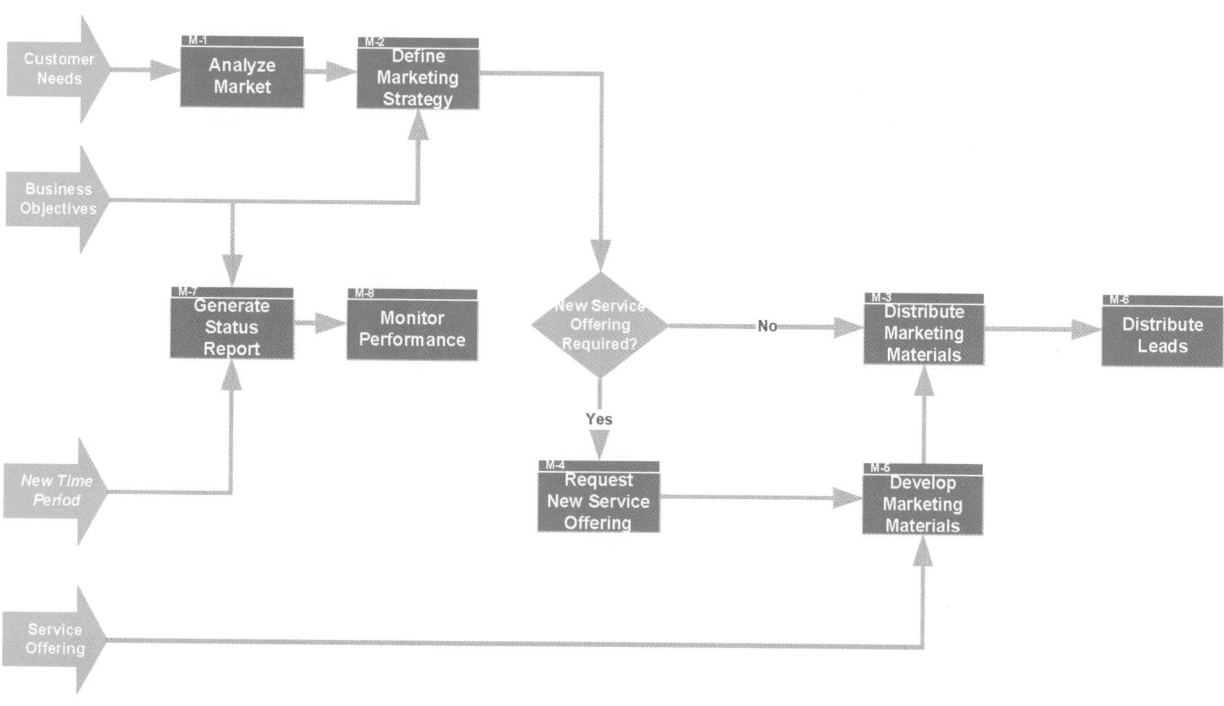

SERVICE DELIVERY

The primary responsibility of Debra our Service Delivery Manager is the delivery of services to clients. Her performance is often measured in terms of customer satisfaction. In order to perform her job well, Debra relies upon information from customers, Sales, and Marketing as well as good resources being provided by HR. These inputs can be summarized as follows:

- Customer Needs
- Sales Orders (Job Numbers)
- New Personnel

The key information packets provided by the Service Delivery organization are as follows:

- Leads
- Case Studies
- Service Offerings
- Timesheets
- Expenses
- Services
- Personnel Requisitions
- Performance Objectives
- Performance Evaluations

The basic information shuffled between Debra and other organizations is portrayed in **Figure 16.**

Debra our Service Delivery Manager starts off her day by reviewing the courtesy newspaper dropped outside of her hotel room door at 5am. The company resource pool has been stretched to the point that she has been deployed on service engagements for some of their higher profile clients. Before going to her client's office, she connects her laptop to the hotel's internet service and is finally able to download her email from the day before. She was unable to do so last night due to the company email server being down. A quick review of her messages reveals that Steve in Sales has landed a few more contracts requiring staffing. Unfortunately, she has no one available to staff the contracts. She has submitted several staff requisitions to Helen in HR, but she has not had time to screen the résumés that Helen has sent to her. Plus, it doesn't look like she will have time until later that evening on the flight back home – after she enters her time and expense information for the past week. She laments the time it takes to gather up her receipts and enter them into spreadsheets that she forwards to Fran in Finance, but failure to complete these mundane administrative tasks results in failure to get paid by her clients. Failure to get paid by clients tends to turn off the lights back in the home office. ▶

Many of the emails in her inbox suggest that she is not the only one lamenting the time and expense entry headaches. Fran is waiting for timesheets and expenses from half of her team covering the past two months. No time to fret over that, though, as she gulps down her breakfast and gets ready for an important meeting with her client. The status report for Mike will have to wait until she has time to type it up on the flight out to the client site next week.

If we were to diagram a typical day in the life of Debra our Service Delivery Manager, it might look something like that shown in **Figure 17.**

Figure 16 Service Delivery SIPOC Model

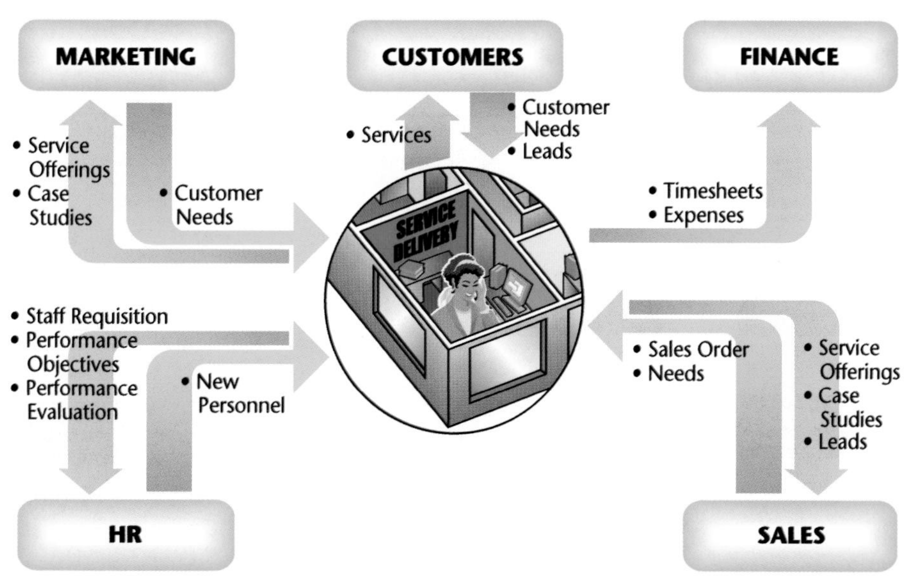

Figure 17 Service Delivery Process Model

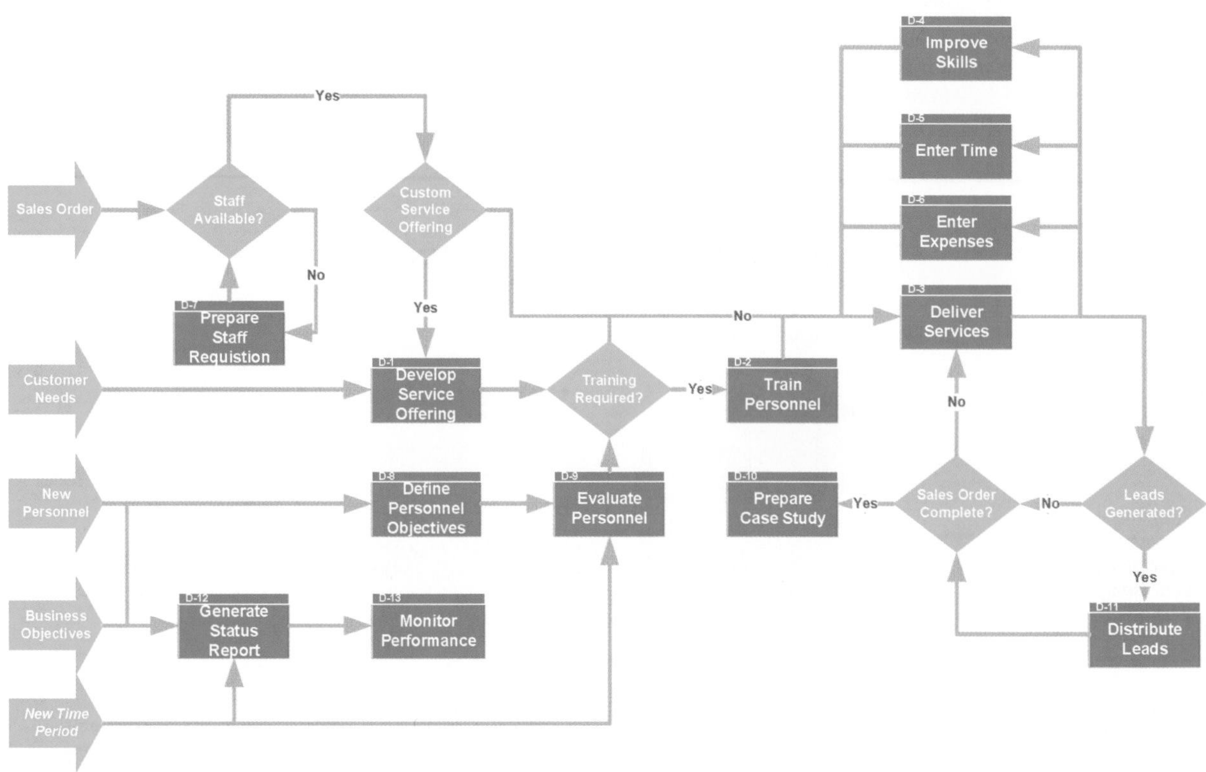

HUMAN RESOURCES

The primary responsibility of Helen our Human Resources Manager is the maintenance of a high-quality resource pool for Service Delivery. Her performance is often measured in terms of employee satisfaction and staff availability in support of service delivery needs. In order to perform her job well, Helen relies upon computers from IT and information from the Service Delivery team. This information can be summarized as:

- Staff Requisitions
- Performance Objectives (Employee Records)
- Performance Evaluations (Employee Records)
- Technology (for equipping new staff)

The key deliverables provided by the human resources organization are:

- New Personnel
- Compensation Profiles
- Technology Requisitions

The basic information shuffled between personnel wearing the human resources hat and other organizations is portrayed in **Figure 18.**

HCM

Human Capital Management software tracks incentives, performance metrics, scheduling/timekeeping, and training for your organization.

Helen our Human Resources Manager starts off her day back in the home office in much the same manner as Steve. She boots up her computer, gets a cup of coffee, and delves into a stream of emails that she has received since leaving the office yesterday. She is vexed by the lack of response by Debra to her requests for résumé screening, but she understands that she is very busy. It looks like she will have to screen the candidates without any inputs from Debra. It has been difficult finding resources that have the skills that are needed by the Service Delivery organization within the necessary salary restrictions. She has managed to find a couple of new employees that she thinks might work out. She has asked Ian to procure two more laptops with the default software profile. Helen conducts a half-day orientation session for the new employees that addresses company policy, benefits, and the expectations associated with their respective roles.

Helen turns her thoughts to existing employees. Bonuses are to be posted at the end of the month, but she has yet to receive any performance evaluations from Debra or her group. This has developed into a pattern over the past year or so. As a result, the bonuses have been distributed evenly throughout the company independent of performance. Many of the better performing personnel are beginning to grumble that this approach is not fair and have quietly begun to float their résumés.

It is Friday, so Helen prepares her status report for Mike in Management. In her report, she cites the new hires as accomplishments. She also feels obligated to cite résumé screening and performance evaluation delays as persistent issues.

If we were to diagram a typical day in the life of Helen our Human Resources Manager, it might look something like that shown in **Figure 19.**

Figure 18 Human Resources SIPOC Model

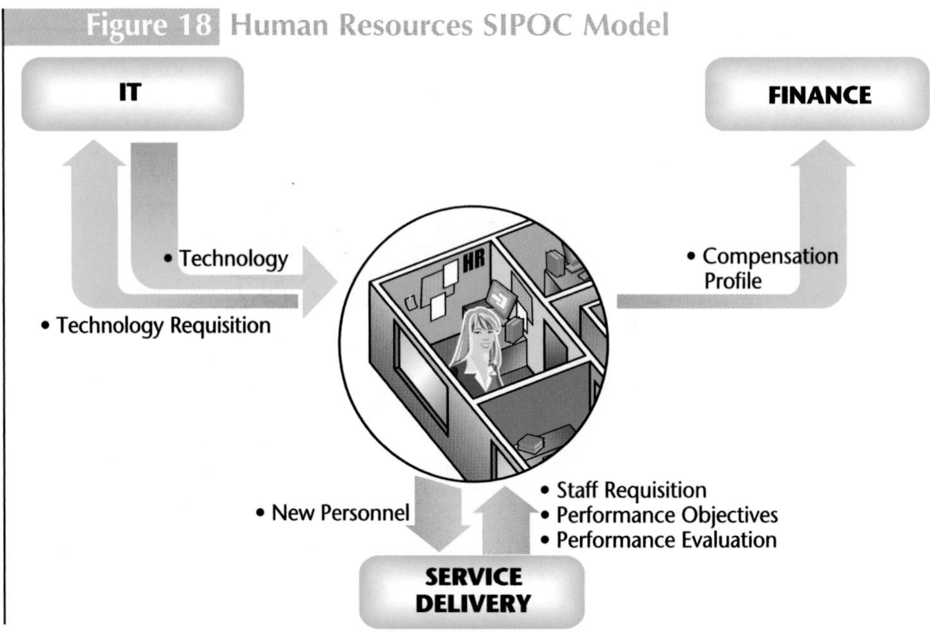

Figure 19 Human Resources Process Model

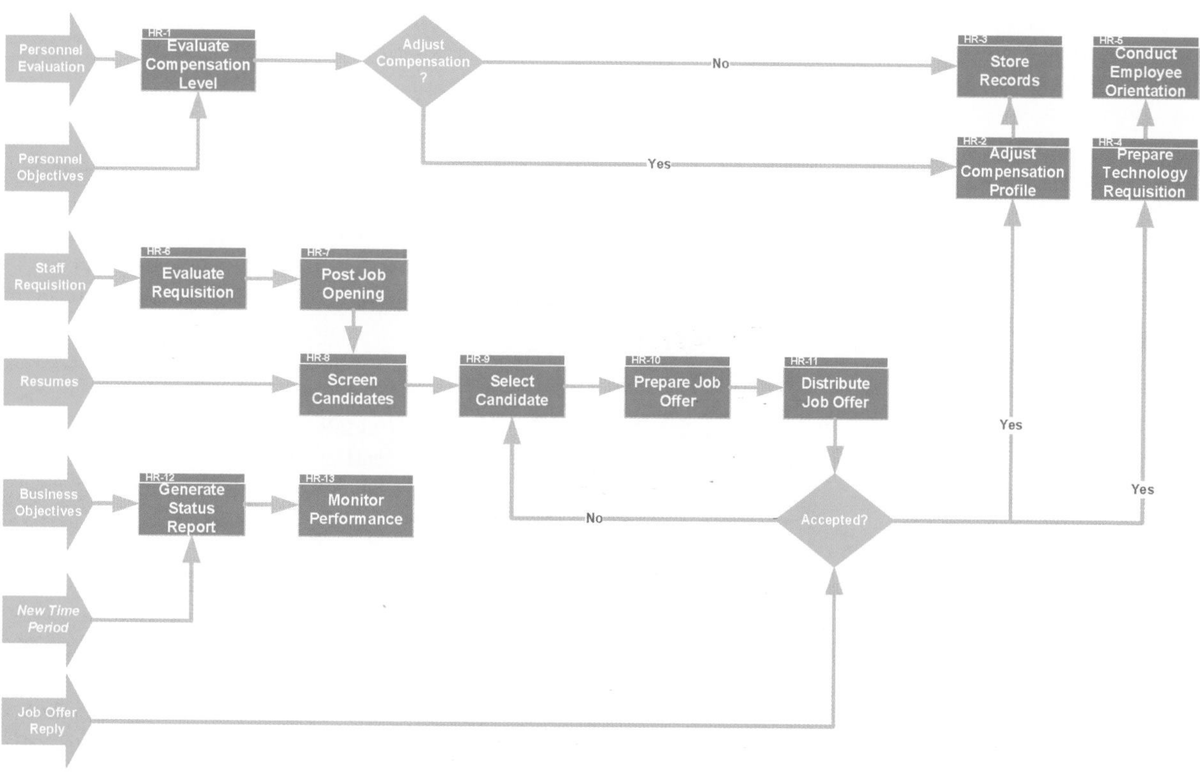

FINANCE

The primary responsibility of Fran our Finance Manager is to manage cash flow. Her performance is often measured in terms of accounts receivable and the accuracy of reports provided to Mike on the management team. In order to perform her job well, Fran relies upon information from HR, customers, suppliers, banks, Sales, and the Service Delivery team. This information can be summarized as follows:

- Payments
- Compensation Profiles
- Withdrawals
- Credit
- Timesheets
- Expenses
- Sales Orders (Job Numbers)
- Bills

The key information packets provided by the finance organization are:

- Payments
- Invoices
- Deposits
- Tax Forms

The basic information shuffled between personnel wearing the finance hat and other organizations is portrayed in **Figure 20.**

Financial Applications

Many financial applications embed services provided by 3rd party service providers. ADP provides payroll services that can link directly to your financial data.

Fran our Finance Manager starts off her day back in the home office in much the same manner as Steve, Mary, and Helen. She boots up her computer, gets a cup of coffee, and delves into a stream of emails that she has received since leaving the office yesterday. Time and expense reports are drifting in from the Service Delivery team. She then turns her attention to regular mail. A host of supplier invoices will have to be routed to her accounts payable specialist and thankfully quite a few customer payments that she will route to her accounts receivable specialist for processing. The Sales and Service Delivery teams have been very diligent in following up with their clients and submitting invoice data such as time and expenses every since Mike had rather forcefully expressed his opinion that the accounts receiv-

Figure 20 Finance SIPOC Model

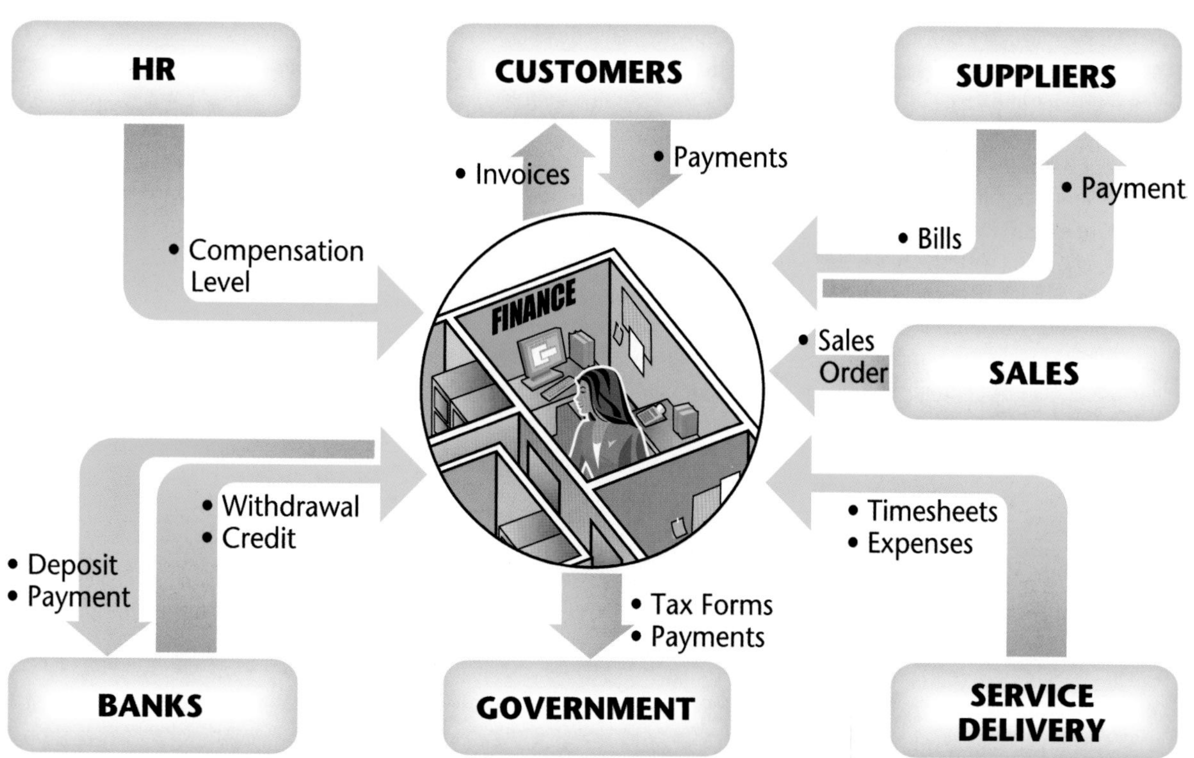

able line item in our Chart of Accounts was excessive and had an adverse impact upon cash flow.

With all of the sales leads in the pipeline, Fran feels it is prudent to investigate extending the line of credit for the company with the bank. She anticipates a delay between when new employees are hired and when they will be available to support a service delivery engagement in a billable capacity. This delay may result in cash flow bumps in the road despite the overall rosy financial performance outlook.

Today is Friday, so Fran also completes her status report for the week. Since it is also the end of the fiscal quarter, she supplements her weekly status report with a full suite of corporate financial reports featuring cash flow statements, income statements, and balance sheets. It has taken her and her staff the better part of two weeks to compile and reconcile all of the information captured in these reports. She is thankful for the breather she has until the next quarterly reporting cycle.

If we were to diagram a typical day in the life of Fran our Finance Manager, it might look something like that shown in **Figure 21.**

Figure 21 Finance Process Model

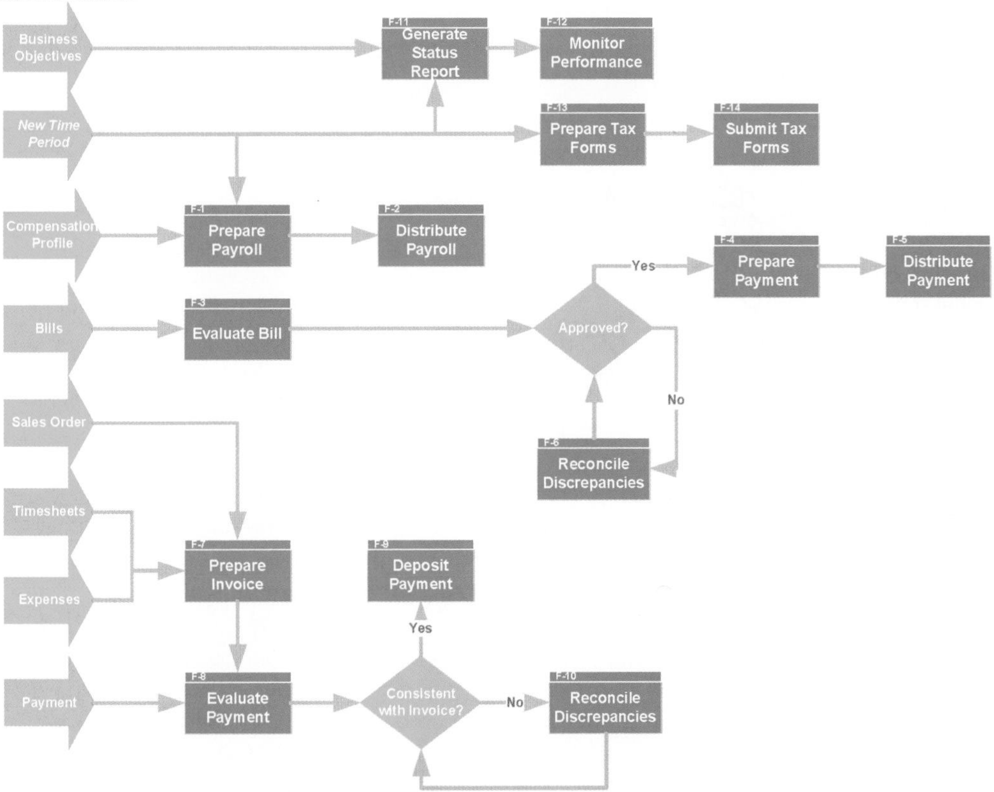

Business Objectives
New Time Period
Compensation Profile
Bills
Sales Order
Timesheets
Expenses
Payment

F-11 Generate Status Report
F-12 Monitor Performance
F-13 Prepare Tax Forms
F-14 Submit Tax Forms
F-1 Prepare Payroll
F-2 Distribute Payroll
F-3 Evaluate Bill
Approved?
Yes
No
F-4 Prepare Payment
F-5 Distribute Payment
F-6 Reconcile Discrepancies
F-7 Prepare Invoice
F-9 Deposit Payment
Yes
F-8 Evaluate Payment
Consistent with Invoice?
No
F-10 Reconcile Discrepancies

INFORMATION TECHNOLOGY

The primary responsibility of Ian our IT Manager is the procurement and maintenance of the company's technology assets, including the company website. His performance is often measured in terms of his responsiveness to technology needs. In order to perform his job well, Ian relies upon information and equipment from Marketing, HR, and his suppliers. These inputs can be summarized as follows:

- Marketing Materials
- Technology Requisitions
- Products
- Services

The key deliverables provided by the IT organization are as follows:

- Purchase Contracts
- Leads (from website)
- Technology (to new staff)

The basic information shuffled between personnel wearing the IT hat and other organizations is portrayed in **Figure 22.**

ITIL

The IT Infrastructure Library (ITIL) is a global industry standard for best practices in IT services that is gaining increased acceptance in the IT community within the U.S. More information on this standard can be found at **www.itil.co.uk.**

Ian the IT Manager starts off his day a little bit later than the rest of the folks in the home office. He had spent most of the night before (and some hours of the early morning) troubleshooting an issue with the mail server caused by a virus and responding to frantic calls from Service Delivery personnel about email access. Now that he has resolved that issue, he has time to respond to Helen's request for additional laptops and software for some new recruits. While he waited for the new computers to arrive, he set them up with some older machines that would provide them with access to the company intranet.

In the hall, Ian bumped into Mike in Management. Mike was excited about a book that he had been reading on IT strategy for small busi- ▶

Figure 22 IT Support SIPOC Model

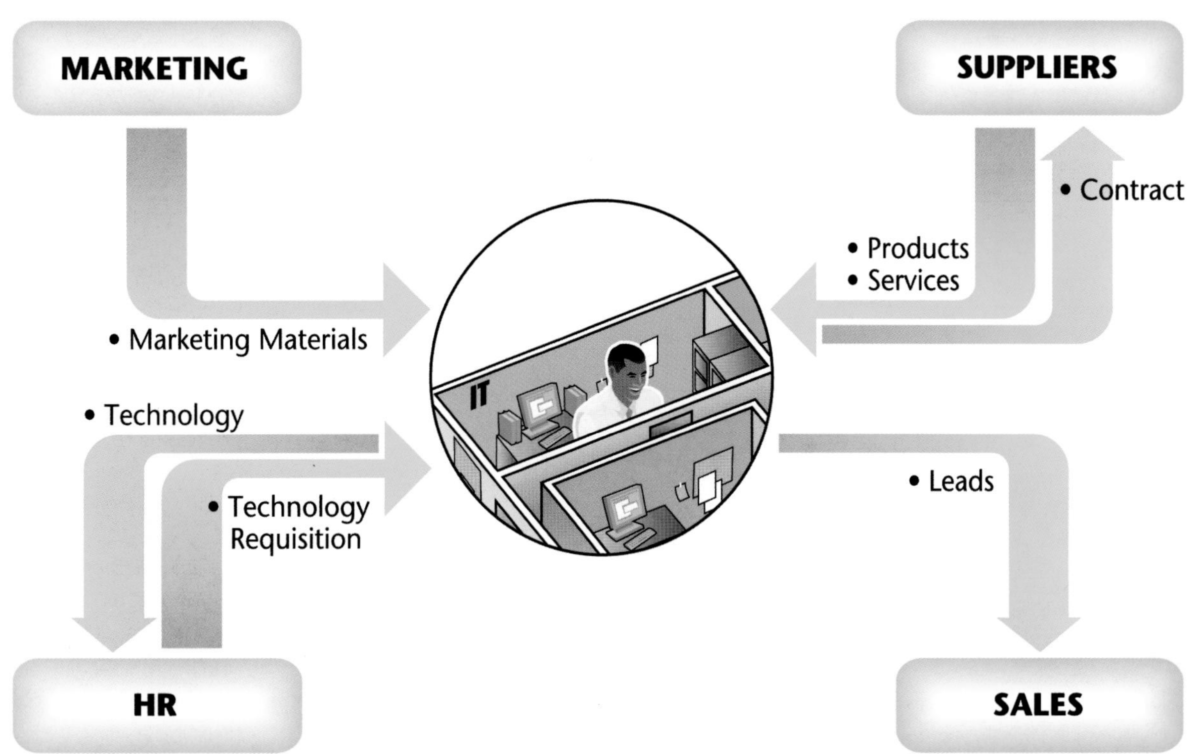

nesses. The book described how IT could move beyond a basic utility for the business and become a key enabler for better business performance. Ian was eager to move beyond a reactive role into a proactive role in the business. Ian took up the challenge of developing an "IT Roadmap" for the business. Since it was Friday, though, he had to take up the challenge of writing up something interesting for his weekly status report to Mike. He had a feeling, though, that it wouldn't be much of a challenge to do so in the coming weeks as his IT Roadmap begins to take shape.

If we were to diagram a typical day in the life of Ian our IT Manager, it might look something like that shown in **Figure 23.**

Figure 23 IT Support Process Model

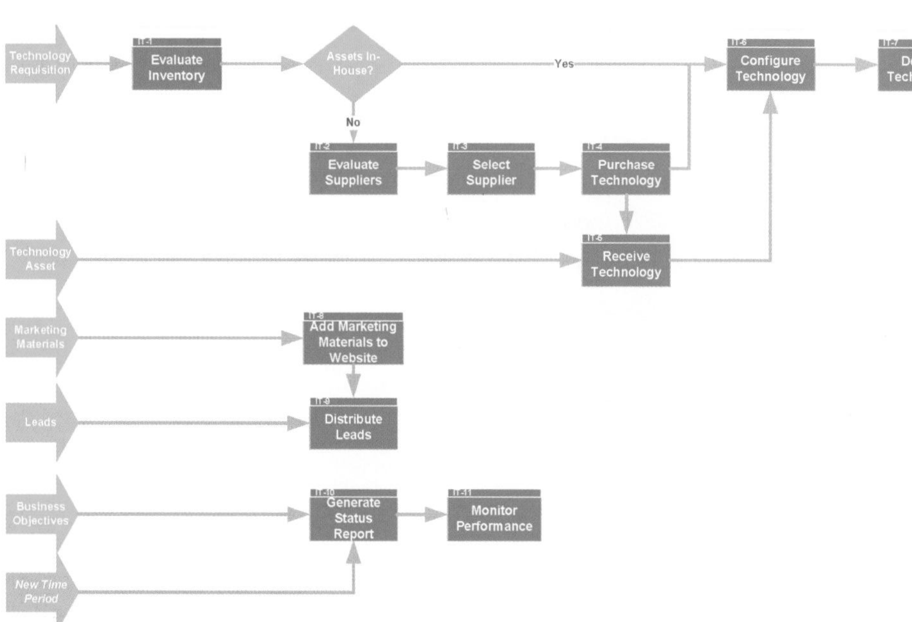

MANAGEMENT

The responsibility of Mike in Management is the overall operation of the business. His performance is often measured in terms of the overall profitability of the business. In order to perform his job well, Mike relies on status reports from every functional organization. In return, Mike is responsible for defining the objectives for each organization in a manner that will improve the overall business performance.

The basic information shuffled between personnel wearing the manager hat and other organizations is portrayed in **Figure 24.**

Mike our General Manager starts off his day with the usual cup of coffee and casual glance through his list of emails. Business was good, but he knew it could be much better. His customers could be happier. His employees could be happier. The business stakeholders such as himself and other partners in the firm could be much happier. He mused to himself, "where should I start?".

BPM

Business Performance Management (BPM) software provides management with centralized access to key information surrounding the performance of their business. Most BPM software provides this information via an easy-to-use web interface.

The status reports from the various managers had begun to trickle in. All indications are that everything was going well except for the Service Delivery organization. It wasn't for lack of effort or skill on the part of Debra and her team. In many ways, they were victims of their own success. The more that they provided excellent services, the more clients wanted those services. The more clients that wanted their services, the more employees they needed to deploy those services. Without time to screen these new employees, there was the risk that new employees would not deliver services with the same quality as before, which would result in a spiral trend in the other direction. There had to be a way to take advantage of current business success and lay the groundwork for a sustainable business model. ▶

Figure 24 Management SIPOC Model

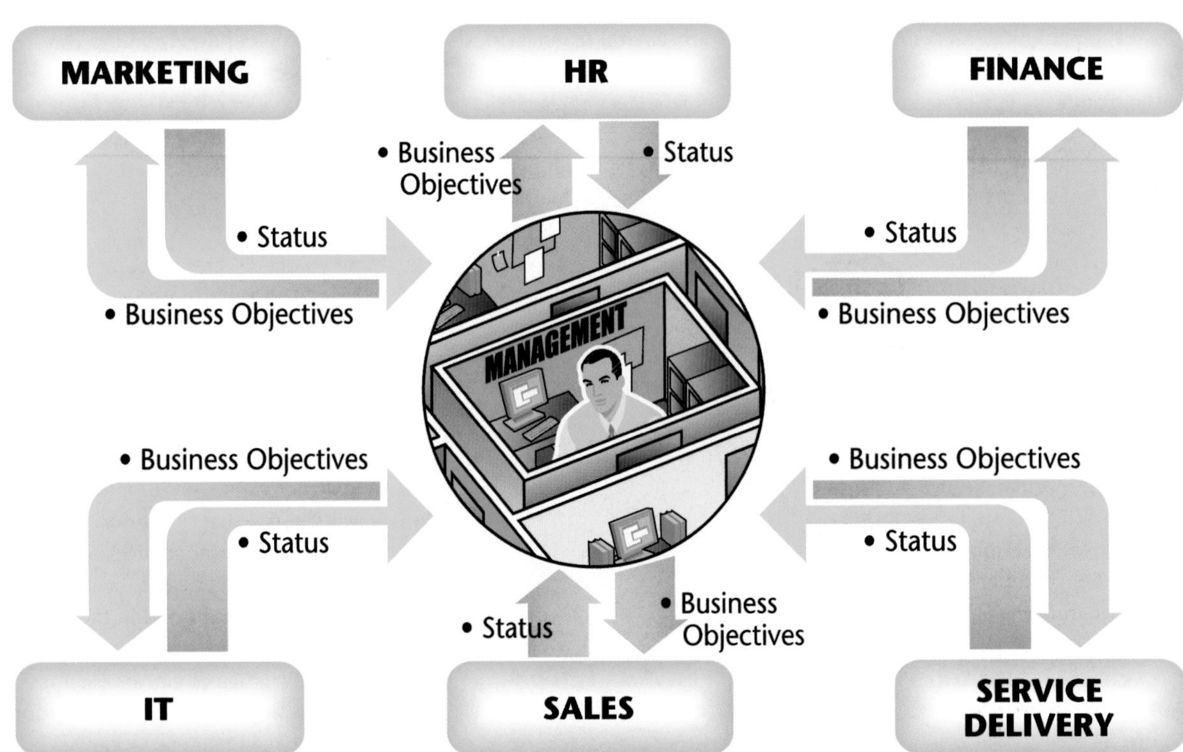

Mike had recently been reading a book called the *IT Roadmap for Professional Service Firms*. He was intrigued by the proposed use of technology to supplement the current business functions rather than become an end in and of itself. He liked the way Superior Services did business and wasn't all that keen about changing the core elements of the company. Clearly, though, something had to change and he decided to ask Ian to put together an IT Roadmap for their business.

If we were to diagram a typical day in the life of Mike our Management Executive, it might look something like that shown in **Figure 25.**

Figure 25 Management Process Model

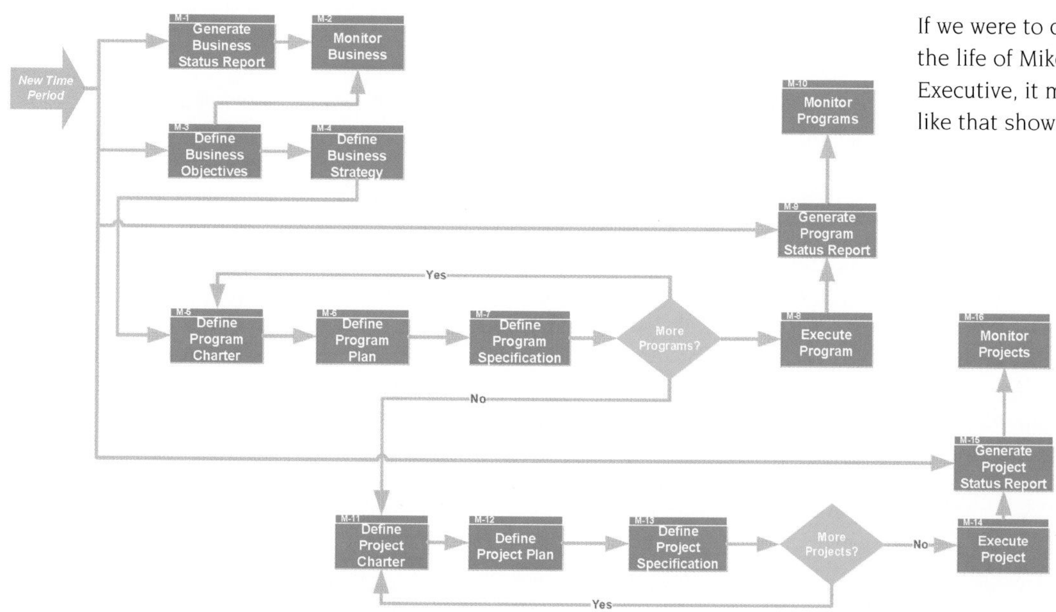

Step 2 Review

In this section, we've organized key aspects of your business and defined how information moves within your organization. The function-based process models layer nicely on top of the functional organization chart that we defined. These relationships are summarized in **Figure 26** and shown from a more detailed perspective later in **Figure 29.** So long as your organization chart remains functionally-based and not name-based, these functional models should scale with your organization. This business model provides us with quite a few insights as to the interdependencies between the different functions within the organization. According to *CIO* magazine, 86% of Chief Information Officer's cite integration-enhancement systems (i.e. tools to connect your business information) and process as the most critical facets of their IT success. The process models that we reviewed in this section are already integrated. If you start off with your business technology and processes already integrated, or a tangible plan on how they will be integrated, you will have a competitive advantage. It is often easier to differentiate than integrate – in business as well as calculus. If you come out of the gates letting each functional organization do their own thing in regards to IT, you will be faced with the significant challenge of integrating these processes and systems later, often at a critical time in your business life. Make it easy on yourself as your business grows – start integrated and stay integrated!

Taken as a whole, these process models provide us with a tangible business model.

With your business model in hand you now have the basis for benchmarking the performance of your current operations. It is very useful to have a solid understanding of where you are starting from before you change to something else. This business model can help eliminate some nasty surprises as your business evolves and seeks to improve its performance. Before we can understand what these performance improvements need to be however, we need in the next step to add some quantifiable attributes to our business model so that we can measure our current performance.

Figure 26 Business Model Overview

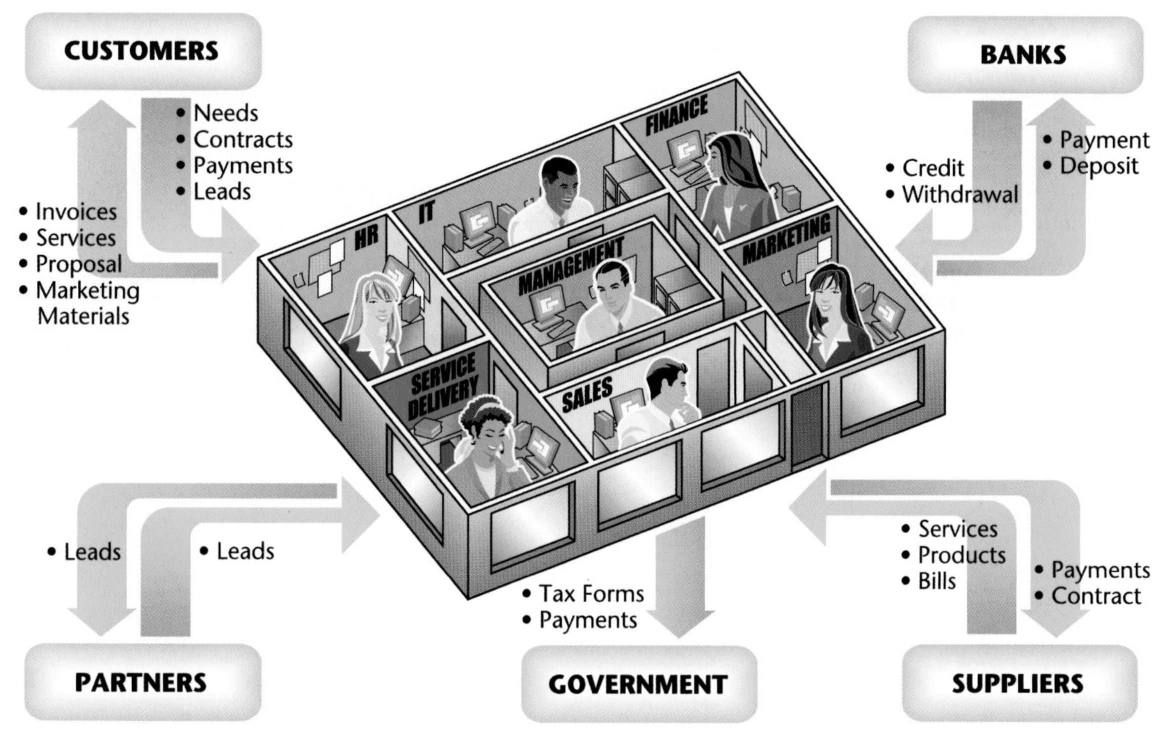

You have now passed by the following IT Roadmap milestones:

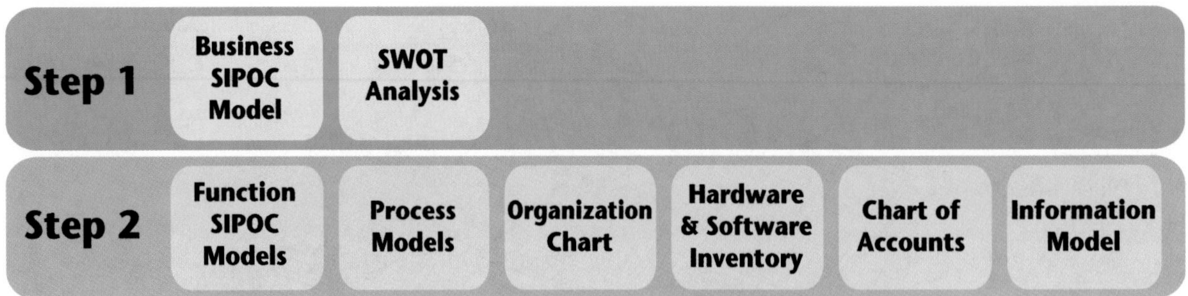

STEP 3: WHERE IS YOUR BUSINESS TODAY?

"Information may be accumulated in files, but it must be retrieved to be of use in decision making".

Kenneth J. Arrow / Nobel Laureate in Economics / *The Limits of the Organization* (Norton, 1974)

Let's up the ante on the question "How do you do it?" and ask "How much does it cost to run your business?" Your IT Roadmap is designed to help you reach new levels of business performance. However, before you begin the climb, you need to know where you are starting. Have you ever found yourself lost while traveling in a strange city or even when wandering around in a strange building? One of the most comforting sights that you might find is a map featuring a reassuring "You are Here" symbol. Wouldn't it be nice to start your journey on the information superhighway with a similar marker? The "Where is your business today?" section provides you with tools that help you to find your position. Once you understand where you are, you will be better equipped to decide upon the best technology route.

Destinations in business come down to numbers. The latitude and longitude of your travel excursions are the expenses and revenue of your business. How easy is it for you to track this information for your business? How often can you determine "where you are"? Monthly? Quarterly? Annually? How far off course might you be before you find out?

The SWOT Analysis in **Step 1** provided you with a bird's eye view of where typical Professional Service Firms find themselves relative to other businesses. The Service Delivery process model discussion in **Step 2** provided some early indicators that all of the cylinders in the business engine of our fictional Superior Services firm may not be working in harmony. Process models by themselves will not provide you with enough information to make a "numbers-based" business case for the products and services of IT vendors. The business overview outlined in **Step 2** defines how you do business, but it does not provide any insights into how well you are doing that business. In order to do so, we need to combine these process models with the cost of resources assigned to tasks within these models. Once this has been done, you will have the IT Roadmap equivalent of a "You are Here" marker.

Expenses

It costs you money to run your business. The salient question in context of our "You are Here" discussion is "How Much?" In our business model, we have defined one example of an integrated suite of functional processes. Each process contains a series of tasks. These tasks hold the key to answering the question "How Much?" Each task has a set of attributes that determines how expensive it is to execute the task. These attributes are summarized in **Figure 27.** Theoretically, you could apply values to these attributes at the process-level of resolution, but you would find yourself taking much larger logic leaps to do so.

The method used for calculating the costs of a task depends upon the type of resources assigned to that task. As was discussed earlier, there are essentially two types of resources that apply to Professional Service Firms – people and technology. People translates into labor expenses while technology translates into material experiences.

LABOR EXPENSES

You may recall the mention of the old adage "time is money". In this section, we get a little bit more formal and convert this adage to a formula. Albert Einstein once said "make it as simple as possible but no simpler", so here we go with the simplest way of expressing "time is money" via a formula:

Labor Cost = Effort x (Labor Rate)

Equation 1

Where:

Effort = (Number of People) x Duration

Equation 2

While this little formula may not be as profound as $E=mc^2$, it may reveal some profound insights into your operations when applied to the process models for your business. It even provides us with some logical insights before we explicitly apply it to our process models. First, the higher the labor rate associated with a resource, the more it will cost to complete tasks to which the resource has been assigned. Second, the greater the effort associated with a task, the higher the cost.

Let's apply these equations to one of the tasks in the Superior Services business model. Since Debra in Delivery looks like she has her hands full in keeping up with the demands of her growing business, we'll delve into a more detailed understanding of one of the tasks in the Service ▶

Figure 27 Task Attributes

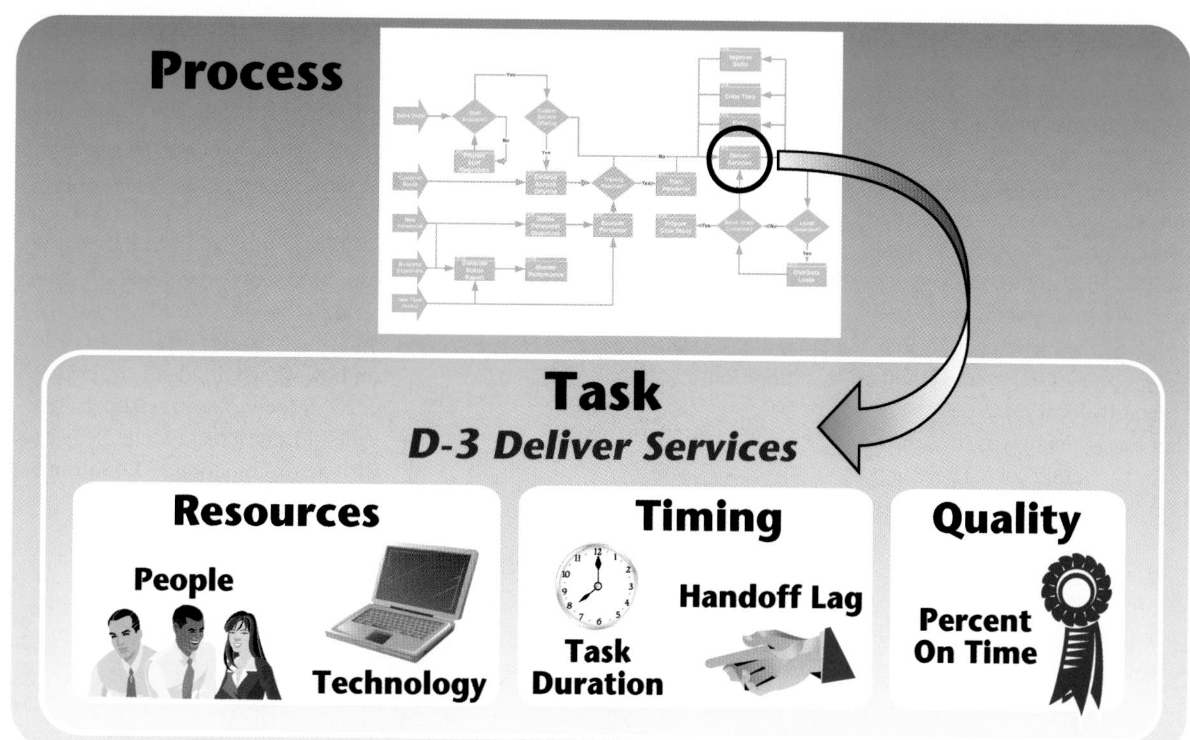

Delivery Process Model depicted in **Figure 17.** The task "D-3 Deliver Service Offering" in the process model seems to get at the heart of Debra's responsibilities. Debra may have multiple instances of this task active at any given time, but let's focus on the instance pertaining to the engagement she is currently supporting.

Let's assume that she is the only resource allocated to the engagement and that her labor rate works out to around $150/hr when you include her salary, bonuses, taxes and standard overhead allocation.

If her engagement were to last two weeks, the total cost for her support of this task is calculated as follows:

Effort = 1 Person x 2 Weeks = 2 Person-Weeks

Labor Cost = 2 Person-Weeks x $150/hr x 40 hr/week = $12,000

Where does this cost get booked? More to the point, which manager visits the hot seat when expenses exceed acceptable levels? Does it get booked to the organization to which the resource is a member or does it get booked to the functional process to which the task is a part? For Superior Services, this is a trivial question because the organization chart for people has the same structure as its business functions. It is not this straightforward in large corporations.

TECHNOLOGY EXPENSES

Independent of the type of organization, however, the tracking of technology costs is not that straightforward. While I have been referring to people as assets, most accountants would beg to differ. The IRS does not generally allow companies to list people as capital assets on tax forms. Technology, though, is a different story and this story has direct implications on how we would ideally track the costs of technology resources. We will start our look at technology costs with an examination of **Equation 3.**

Technology Costs = (Deployment Costs + Operating Costs) x % Total Cost Allocation

Equation 3

Where:

Deployment Costs = Deployment Project Labor Costs + Software Licensing Costs (Initial users) + Hardware Procurement Costs

Equation 4

And:

Operating Costs = [IT Support Labor Costs + Software Licensing Costs (Upgrades + Incremental users) + Hardware Maintenance Costs] x Duration of Task

Equation 5

The first step in determining the expenses incurred by assigning an off-the-shelf technology solution to a task is to determine the overall cost of a given technology resource.

Once we have calculated the total cost of the technology, we need to determine what percentage of this cost should be allocated to supporting a given task. The simplest and often fairest model would be to allocate costs on the basis of the number of tasks associated with the technology as described in **Equation 6.**

% Total Cost Allocation = 1/(Total Number of Tasks to Which Technology has Been Allocated) x 100%

Equation 6

While it is possible to derive some rather sophisticated models for the allocation of costs to specific tasks on the basis of the number of users associated with a given task, CPU demand and the like, let's keep things as simple as possible. We can still draw some very useful conclusions about our cost drivers even with a simple model. First, the cost of technology is independent of the time ▶

Task Trend

The trend towards task-resolution software applications in support of Service Oriented Architectures would indicate that task-based approach towards allocating technology costs should prove to be a stable approach over the years. The business case for adding task-based software programs to your technology portfolio would be easy to generate. Simply compare the cost of the program to the cost of the labor that would otherwise be required.

it takes to execute a task. Second, the more tasks to which a given technology is allocated, the lower the cost per task.

Let's take a further look at the costs of executing task D-3 and see how much it costs to provide the technology necessary to support the task. Let's assume that the only technology that Debra needs to support her client is a laptop running the Windows XP Operating System and Microsoft Office Professional. The technology expense might work out as follows:
Deployment Costs = 0.5 hr x $80/hr + $600 + $2,000 = $2,640
Operating Costs = ($80,000/yr + $250/yr + $1,000/yr) x (80hr/2,080 hr/yr) = $3,125
% Total Cost Allocation = 1/100 = 0.01
Technology Costs = ($2,640 + $3,125) x 0.01 = $57.65
Therefore, the total expenses (both labor and technology) needed to support the execution of task D-3 are $12,057.65, with the bulk of the expenses going to labor. Regarding the $12,057.65, where does this cost get booked? Does it get booked to IT or does it get booked to the functional process to which the task that features the resource assignment is part? If you simply allocate your costs to IT, you will not be able to track the true cost of executing your business model. In this light, it is best to allocate your costs to the functional process in which the technology finds itself used. All of this bookkeeping implies that you have discipline on another bookkeeping front – when you deploy the software. We will be addressing this discipline in **Step 5.**

Independent of how we book the costs, we now have expense information that is much more useful in making decisions than the cost information you would find in a traditional Chart of Accounts. You now have information that will enable you to go beyond looking for big numbers in your Chart of Accounts and slashing budget allocations to that line item. With your task-level expense information, you can determine where you can make performance improvements that last beyond a single financial reporting cycle.

Revenue

OK...enough with spending money. Businesses are about making money! Let's take a look at how we can model revenue in our business. From the bird's eye view of the business, tracking revenue is pretty straightforward. The payments that we receive from our customers yield revenue. What happens within the walls of our business? Are some functions more responsible for revenue than others? Of course, some will say it is obvious that Sales is the organization ultimately responsible for revenue. Our process parable about lost nails suggests that it might be a bit more complicated than this supposition. If there is no Service Delivery, there is no work for which we can bill the client. Without HR, there would be no staff to deliver the services. Without Finance and payroll, there would be no one except for interns. Without IT, there would be no need for this book! We clearly need to take a closer look at the movement of money within our business model.

Two fundamental approaches to tracking revenue exist. One either treats functional organizations as cost centers or profit centers. Cost centers take the bird's eye approach of looking at revenue only from the perspective of the business as a whole. Budget plans for functional organizations within the business only look at the expense line items in the General Ledger. Profit centers treat each functional organization as a mini-business in and of itself. Budget plans resemble supplier contracts in that they address the value of deliverables to be provided and the costs associated with those deliverables. Ostensibly, most "profit centers" would be more akin to "non-profit centers" to preclude taking profit for one organization at the expense of another organization. Properly regulated, however, profit could be used to measure the relative efficiency of each functional organization. A summary of the relative benefits and disadvantages of each approach is provided in **Table 7.**

You can take either the Cost Center or Profit Center approach and still develop a working IT Roadmap. The key information that you need is an understanding of how the revenue bone is connected to the expense bone. Revenue targets without a reasonable understanding of what it takes to reach those targets can amount to pure fantasy. In Professional Service Firms, higher revenue depends upon one or more of the following set of metrics: ▶

- Increased % of billable time
- Increased number of employees
- Higher rates

Each of these metrics has a cost side of the equation. Higher percentages of billable time can lead to burnout and less time for employees to improve or share their skills with other employees. These situations result in higher employee turnover and virtual debits from your firm's intellectual capital account. Increasing the number of employees results in additional labor expenses and provides additional task loads upon their managers and support organizations such as HR, IT and Finance. Higher rates typically imply one of two things: you have moved into a new market that is generally naïve in regards to typical rates for your services or you have created a new service offering that differentiates you from your competition. Moving into a new market implies additional costs associated with advertising, tailored marketing materials, and perhaps additional sales personnel. The development of new service offerings requires time and, as discussed earlier, time is money.

Table 7 / Cost Centers vs. Profit Centers

Approach	Benefits	Disadvantages
Cost Centers	All operating costs for a given functional department are fairly self-contained. Budget planning for each department only needs to address expenses.	Does not provide each organization with a sense of their contribution to the revenue side of the ledger.
Profit Centers	Tangible understanding of the performance of each organization Provides ability to focus your business on core competencies and outsource the rest. Enables better benefit-cost project funding allocations.	Very difficult to establish without a process-based business model. May discourage collaboration between functional departments unless performance metrics encourage such collaboration.

Scorecards

In the end, revenue must exceed expenses, or before long you will be getting visits from a very special type of moving company. Your company financial reports provide you with a tracking mechanism to avoid these special visits. Balance Sheets track assets against liabilities. Cash Flow reports track revenue against expenses for a given time period. Traditionally, these financial reports take weeks to generate and weeks to analyze. In order to make decisions quickly, we need to have information presented to us in a manner that makes better use of our time. Rather than having to sift through a sea of financial statements, it would be nice if we could zero in on the information that needs our attention and ignore the information that does not need our consideration.

Let's step out of our discussion about virtual roadmaps and take a peek at our experience driving on a real road. Imagine what driving would be like if we were to replace stop lights with billboards of information pertaining to the crash specifications of popular vehicles and the impacts of exceeding certain parameters in the specifications to personnel traveling in the vehicle. Somehow the idea of simply braking when the light is red and continuing on with what you were doing when it is green seems a bit more appealing. Why should it be any different for your business?

Traffic lights can be as useful for our business as they are for managing road traffic. We need indicators that tell us when it is time to stop and take a closer look or to keep on going without a care in the world. Where would we place these traffic lights in your business? One place that makes sense is at the entrance to our business. This traffic light would be responsible for letting us know how well the business is performing in regards to revenue and expenses. This information might be represented in a scorecard akin to that in **Figure 28.**

Where else might we place scorecards? How about outside the offices of each of our functional organizations? We could track the financial performance of these organizations as well, now that we know how much their functions cost. We may also be interested in tracking additional information specific to that function. **Table 8** provides a sample list of key performance indicators that might be useful to track for each of our functional organizations.

Figure 28 Sample Business Scorecard

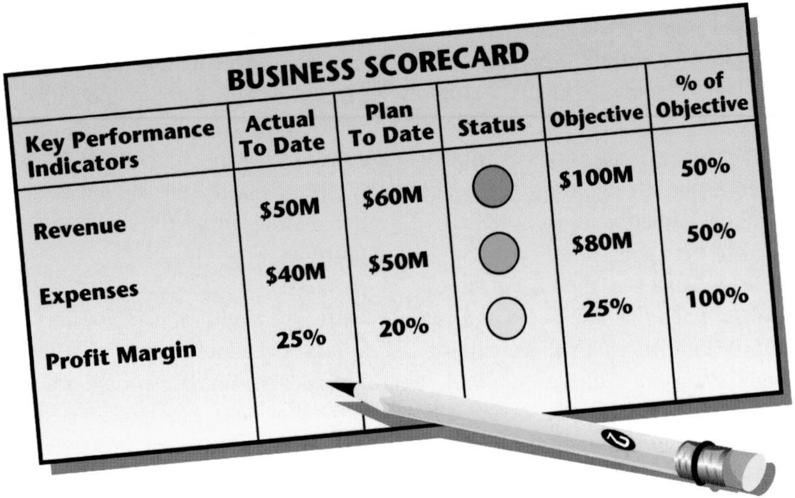

BUSINESS SCORECARD

Key Performance Indicators	Actual To Date	Plan To Date	Status	Objective	% of Objective
Revenue	$50M	$60M		$100M	50%
Expenses	$40M	$50M		$80M	50%
Profit Margin	25%	20%		25%	100%

Table 8 / Key Performance Indicators

Function	Key Performance Indicators
Sales	Revenue, Lead Closure Rate, Cost of Sales
Marketing	# Leads, % Qualified Leads
Service Delivery	Schedule Variance, Cost Variance, Job Profitability, Customer Satisfaction
Human Resources	Employee Turnover Rate, Open Job Requisitions, Resource Quality
Finance	Average Receiveables Age, Cash Flow Margin
IT	System Down Time, Issue Response Time, Issue Resolution Time, Employee Satisfaction
Management	Profitability, Revenue, Expenses, Growth Rate

Step 3 Review

This section has connected metrics to money and money to processes to establish a means of determining "where you are" with your business. Now we are faced with the challenge of how to establish an achievable performance objective. How many times have you been in organizations where an edict comes down from on high to cut expenses by 10%? Cutting expenses by 10% is an easily identifiable goal. Most companies are forced to take this approach because they lack the information necessary to take a more surgical approach. We, on the other hand, have been building an information store that will enable this surgical approach. In the next section, we'll put that information to use.

You have now passed by the following IT Roadmap milestones:

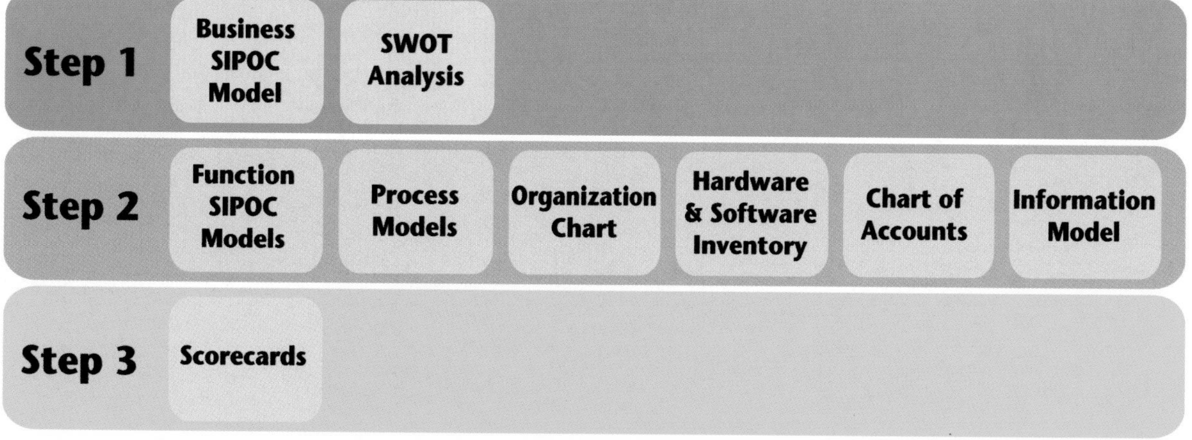

STEP 4: WHERE DO YOU WANT YOUR BUSINESS TO BE?

"Ready. ...Fire. ...Aim." Unsuccessful Hunter

How many times have businesses sounded the following call: reduce expenses by 10%, and do it quickly. An objective of this sort typically inspires a search through the General Ledger to find the expense line item with the biggest number (e.g. travel and entertainment expenses) followed by a mandate to cut that line item until you reach the 10% threshold. For awhile, staff focuses on reducing those expenses, but, as time goes by, everyone takes their eye off the ball and the line item drifts back into old form. Wouldn't it be nice if these "fire drills" could be replaced by something that creates lasting change?

In order to achieve lasting change, you first need to target lasting change. Saying that you're ready to change and pulling the trigger to change are fairly easy compared to actually taking the time to figure out what you need to hit. Long-range "aiming" takes a sniper's discipline to be effective. Unfortunately, the weapon of choice for taking out targets in business is a shotgun. A shotgun is easy to aim and the chances of hitting short range targets are fairly good, but try to hit a long-range target with same weapon and you'll be disappointed. Unlike a rifle, which precisely fires a single bullet at a particular target, a shotgun will spray pellets over a wide area. The further away the target is, the larger the area over which the shot spreads, so, if you're trying to hit a small target at a long distance, only a fraction of your pellets will hit the intended target. What happens to the pellets that miss their target? Often they strike unintentional targets. The same thing can happen to your business if you use a shotgun rather than a rifle to hit your long-range performance targets.

One example of a shotgun objective is a management decree for each functional department to reduce expenses by 10%. What would the functional managers at Superior Services do if Mike were inclined to require a 10% across-the-board cut in expenses? If we were to assume that HR, IT and Finance staffing levels are equal to what's needed, Helen, ▶

Ian, and Fran would be forced to evaluate pay cuts, benefit cuts, or investigate outsourcing. Sales, Marketing, and Service Delivery might also look at such areas, but Steve, Mary, and Debra would have a few more options such as lower-cost travel, bypassing marketing events, or reducing client perks. All of these options have one common feature – they satisfy short-range objectives, but they sacrifice long-range performance.

One of the reasons managers have made shotguns the weapon of choice is that they have limited ammunition suitable for longer-range targets. Management's ammunition is information. In the realm of financial performance, most managers are limited to General Ledger reports driven by a traditional Chart of Accounts. We have already cited the shortcomings of these reports. Once you build your IT Roadmap, you will be able to supplement your arsenal of decision-making information with a very powerful business tool made practical courtesy of the Information Age. This tool is your business model.

Your business model will enable you to define your financial performance objectives in a way that connects these objectives to the people and processes that will be instrumental in achieving those objectives. When you combine organization with process models and resources as summarized in **Figure 29,** you have answers to some of the most complex questions about your business. This business model contains the information decision makers need in order to make effective decisions. By connecting your objectives to a "day in the life" of your employees rather than a sometimes arbitrary entry in the Chart of Accounts, you will be laying the groundwork for changes that stand the test of time. Wouldn't it be nice to look for new opportunities to improve the business rather than replaying the same old fire drills? In this section, we will explore new targets of opportunity. There truly is gold in 'dem 'der hills. Our goal is to find out where that gold is and box it up so that it can be put to good use for longer than a single management review. We are going to center our exploration on what will be referred to as value streams. Each of these value streams contains nuggets that can be used to finance the road to our eventual business destination.

Figure 29 Detailed Business Model

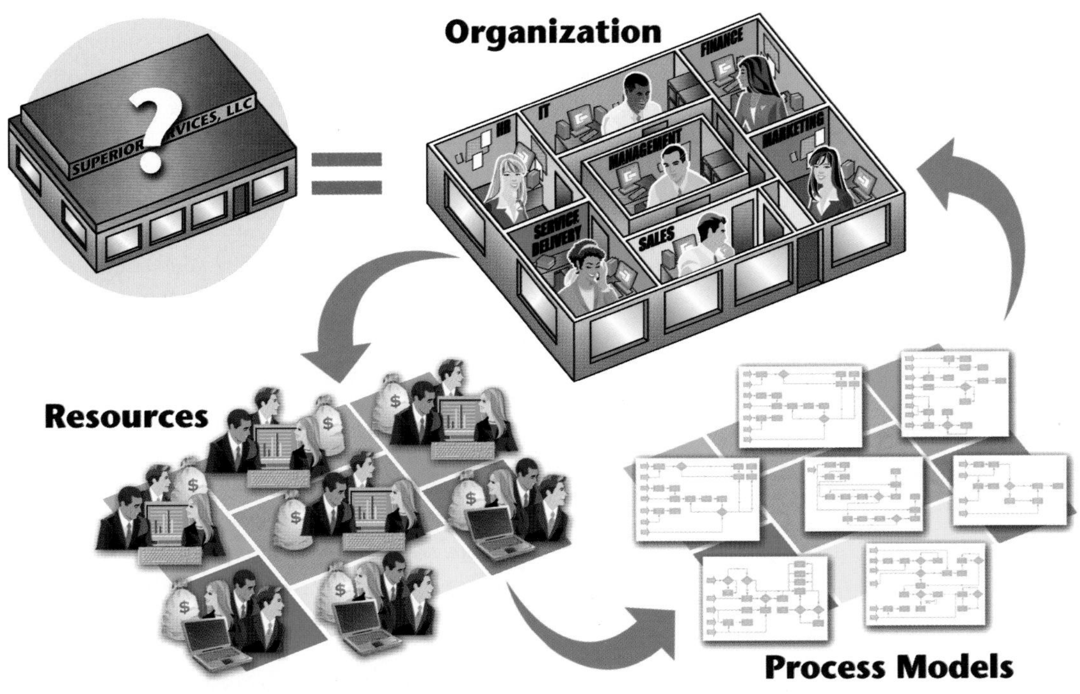

Value Streams

What is a value stream? Value streams are a select group of tasks that heavily influence the performance of one or more areas of your business. The purpose of value streams is to provide you with a quick method of evaluating the benefit of pursuing a certain business improvement strategy. One of the key reasons to use value streams is their ability to simplify the analysis of what can be a complex set of business processes. The functional models that make up your business model work well for training, audits, and general expectation management, but they can be overwhelming if you attempt to analyze them collectively. The concept of value streams allows us to break our processes down into smaller chunks and focus our aim more precisely on high impact returns.

Value Streams
Value Streams enable you to filter out the clutter and focus on a select few of the hundreds of tasks in your overall business model.

Value streams provide you with the flexibility to look beyond a single process model and examine dependencies between different functions at a task level. As depicted in **Figure 30,** the tasks for a given value stream are extracted from one or more existing process models. The criteria for selecting tasks depend upon the performance that you are attempting to improve. If you are attempting to improve customer satisfaction, you should select tasks that influence the customer's perception of your firm. If you are attempting to improve the appearance of your company to a potential investor, you should isolate those tasks that have the most impact on your balance sheet. The tasks that are selected for a given value stream should have a direct influence on the performance area under consideration.

What, specifically, are some of the value streams in your business? If many value streams are hidden in the process flows that make up our business model, where do you start? One way of getting the ball rolling for Professional Service Firms is to ask, "What perspectives matter most in your business?" Most Professional Service Firms are driven by the

Figure 30 Creating a Value Stream

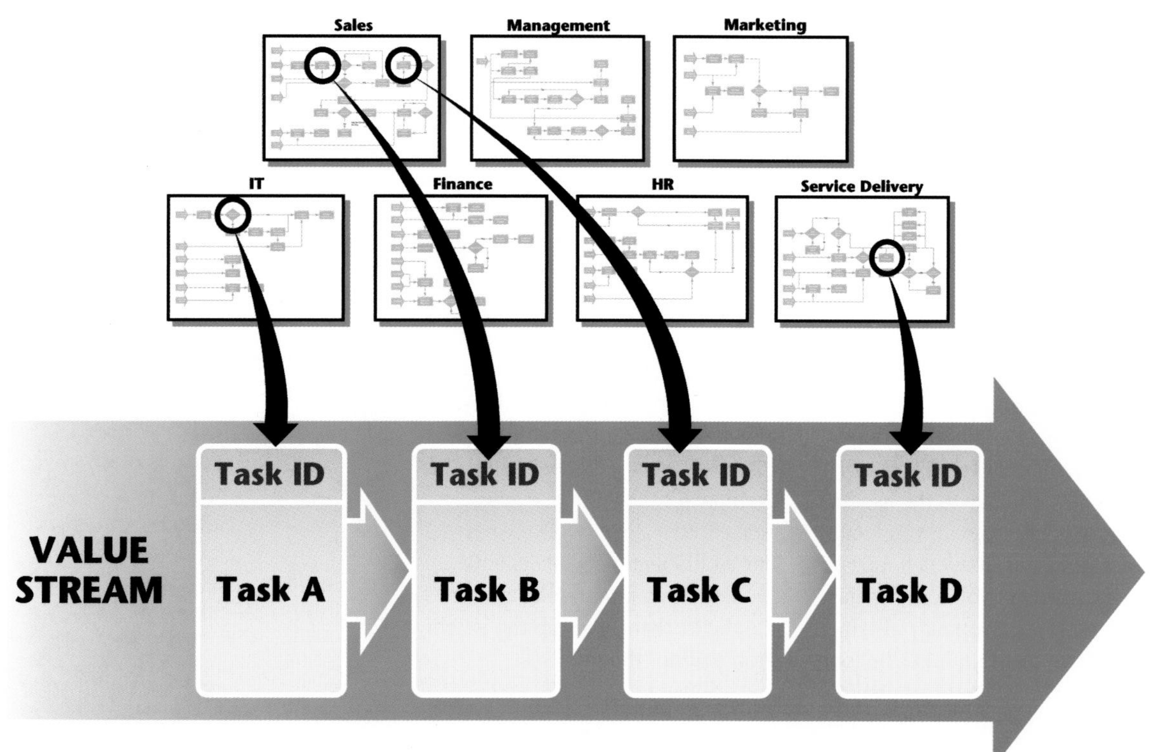

perceptions of the following groups:

- **Stakeholders:** People with a financial stake in the company such as partners
- **Customers:** People willing to pay you for your services
- **Employees:** The people who provide the services

Each of these important groups brings a different focus and a different set of values to the assessment of your vision. If you focus on making stakeholders happy at the exclusion of your customers and employees, you may obtain short-term gains and risk the long-term viability of your company. If you focus on making your customers happy at the exclusion of your employees and stakeholders, you may be the recipient of significant unwanted attention from your creditors. If you focus on making your employees happy at the exclusion of your stakeholders and customers, your employees may find that they would be most happy if they would be paid on a regular basis. At times, these perspectives may yield conflicting performance goals. For example, stakeholders would like to maximize billable time while clients would like to minimize costs. Conflicts, thankfully, are the exception and not the rule.

Balanced Scorecards

The concept of a balanced scorecard was formalized as a management methodology in the early 1990's by Dr. David Norton and Dr. Robert Kaplan. The basic premise of this methodology holds that management actions should be viewed from a prism featuring the following perspectives: Financial, Customer, Internal Business Processes, and Learning and Growth. The principle benefit of this approach is to ensure that the long-term implications of management decisions are considered in conjunction with what are often short-term financial goals.

For each of the three value streams we identified above, we will look at three basic metrics: duration, cost, and quality. Duration is simply how long a single instance of the task may take to complete. Cost is a total of the labor and technology expenses for a given task as covered in **Step 3.** Quality focuses on answering the reliability-based questions such as "Did the task start on time?" and "Did the task finish on time?" In a Professional Service Firm, reliability is treasured not only by your customers, but also by your own employees. Fran's Finance troops cannot submit invoices on time unless they receive time and expense reports from Debra's Delivery troops. The initial values for these metrics can be estimated on the basis of experience or entered as a result of formal time studies. The former approach will work just fine provided that the individual providing the estimate has experience performing the task in question. For simplicity, we will assume that each task in a given value stream occurs only once per review cycle. You may wish to use different metrics or apply different weights to each task within your model.

With this information in hand, we will be able to define a sample value stream for each of them. With the value streams defined, we will look for the opportunities or "nuggets" in each stream. Once we isolate the opportunities in each value stream, we will be able to define achievable objectives for each value stream that will be put to use in **Step 5.** Let's now take a look at what drives the satisfaction of each of these perspectives.

Value Stream Management

The origins of Value Stream Management trace back to manufacturing process improvement. Engineers are constantly seeking ways to improve the efficiency of manufacturing operations. Their definition of Value Stream is "a collection of all the steps (both value-added and non-value added) involved in bringing a product or group of products from raw material to finished products accepted by a customer".

(SOURCE: Value Stream Management, p. 152)

STAKEHOLDERS

What do stakeholders value? Higher profit is the key to happier stakeholders. It often indicates the degree to which they benefit financially from the performance of the company. Three basic ways of tackling higher profit are: increase revenue, decrease expenses or some combination thereof. A peek under the hood of our business model indicates that many ways of increasing revenue or decreasing expenses can potentially be found. As a means of getting started, let's isolate a single value stream within this sea of possibilities. Service Delivery efficiency would seem to have the greatest impact on profitability. Debra our Service Delivery Manager seems to have a lot on her plate. Perhaps this focus would also lend itself to some improvements that might lighten her load.

The key activities associated with delivering services for Superior Services are summarized in **Figure 31.** These tasks have been extracted from the service delivery and finance process models.

Figure 31 Stakeholder Value Stream

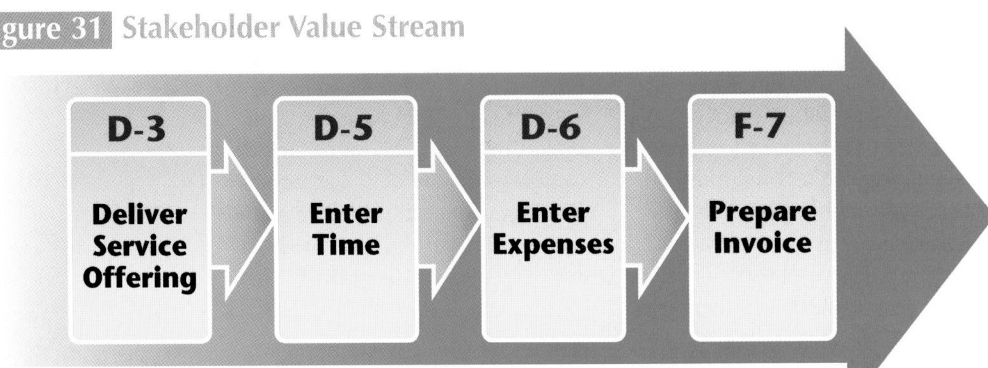

The keys to increasing profitability are to maximize the revenue gained from delivering a service and to minimize the costs. If a service is provided on a time and material basis, you achieve peak revenue by maximizing your billable time. If a service is provided on a fixed price basis, you will need to focus on reducing the cost of delivery in order to improve profitability. The cost of delivery is the cost of the activities involved in providing services to the client and billing the client for these services and associated expenses. Let's calculate the current cost of delivery for these tasks using the equations that we introduced in **Step 3**.

Table 9 / Stakeholder Value Stream Metrics

Task ID	D-3			D-5			D-6			F-7			TOTALS
Task Description	**Deliver Service Offering**			**Enter Time**			**Enter Expenses**			**Prepare Invoice**			
Timing													
Task Duration	160		hrs	0.25		hrs	2		hrs	0.5		hrs	163
Handoff Lag Time	0		hrs	0		hrs	0		hrs	0		hrs	0
Total Time	160		hrs	0.25		hrs	2		hrs	0.5		hrs	163
Quality													
% On-Time Start	50%			100%			100%			50%			25%
% On-Time Finish	50%			100%			100%			50%			25%
Expenses													
Labor Expenses	*# Heads*		*Rate*	*# Heads*		*Rate*		*# Heads*	*Rate*		*# Heads*	*Rate*	
Senior Staff	1		$ 150	1		$ 150	1		$ 150	1		$ 150	
Administrative Support	0.25		$ 50	0		$ 50	0		$ 50	0.25		$ 50	
Labor Subtotal			*$ 26,000*			*$ 38*			*$ 300*			*$ 81*	*$ 26,419*
Technology	*Deploy*	*Ops*	*% Alloc*	*Deploy*	*Ops*	*% Alloc*	*Deploy*	*Ops*	*% Alloc*	*Deploy*	*Ops*	*% Alloc*	
Windows XP	$ 2,240	$ 3,119	0.01	$ 2,240	$ 3,119	0.01	$ 2,240	$ 3,119	0.01	$ 2,240	$ 3,119	0.01	
MS Office	$ 440	$ 3,083	0.01	$ 440	$ 3,083	0.01	$ 440	$ 3,083	0.01	$ 440	$ 3,083	0.01	
Technology Subtotal			*$ 54*			*$ 54*			*$ 54*			*$ 54*	*$ 214*
Total Expenses			*$ 26,054*			*$ 91*			*$ 354*			*$ 135*	*$ 26,633*

Where are the value stream improvement opportunities amidst the values in **Table 9**? Each cell in **Table 10** offers potential improvement opportunities. What if we were to pursue a fixed price revenue model? Superior Services could package some of the more administrative service offerings for delivery via the web and generate revenue without the need to deploy staff to the client site. This approach might lighten the load on Debra and her staff without adversely impacting revenue. On the cost side of the ledger, how could we reduce the time spent supporting non-billable activities? We could reduce the time spent by Debra and her staff entering expense information by using credit cards with smart tracking features that allow lower-cost administrative support personnel to prepare the bulk of the expense report data and relegate the senior staff to review and approval time. We could provide administrative staff in Fran's organization with access to centralized timesheet and expense data and allow them to generate invoices. Debra and her staff would only need to devote time to the review and approval of invoices prior to Fran's team sending the invoice to the client. These opportunities have been highlighted in **Table 10**.

Whether or not we decide to pursue the solutions suggested above, we now have the basis for defining an achievable objective for the value stream. Between the time you define your objectives and the time to begin work to achieve them, you may find even better approaches to reaching the objectives. At this point in the construction of your IT Roadmap, we are focused on defining what could be done, not how it will be done.

Table 10 / Stakeholder Value Stream Opportunities

Task ID	D-3			D-5			D-6			F-7			TOTALS
Task Description	**Deliver Service Offering**			**Enter Time**			**Enter Expenses**			**Prepare Invoice**			
Timing													
Task Duration		0	hrs		0.25	hrs		1	hrs		0.5	hrs	2
Handoff Lag Time		0	hrs		0	hrs		0	hrs		0	hrs	0
Total Time		0	hrs		0.25	hrs		1	hrs		0.5	hrs	2
Quality													
% On-Time Start			50%			100%			100%			50%	25%
% On-Time Finish			50%			100%			100%			50%	25%
Expenses													
Labor Expenses	# Heads		Rate	# Heads		Rate		# Heads	Rate		# Heads	Rate	
Senior Staff		1	$ 150		1	$ 150		1	$ 150		0.1	$ 150	
Administrative Support		0.25	$ 50		0	$ 50		0	$ 50		1	$ 50	
Labor Subtotal			$ -			$ 38			$ 150			$ 33	$ 220
Technology	Deploy	Ops	% Alloc	Deploy	Ops	% Alloc	Deploy	Ops	% Alloc	Deploy	Ops	% Alloc	
Windows XP				$ 2,240	$ 3,119	1%	$ 2,240	$ 3,119	1%	$ 2,240	$ 3,119	1%	
MS Office				$ 440	$ 3,083	1%	$ 440	$ 3,083	1%	$ 440	$ 3,083	1%	
Small Business Server	$ 3,240	$ 6,238	100%	$ 440	$ 3,083	1%	$ 440	$ 3,083	1%	$ 440	$ 3,083	1%	
Technology Subtotal			$ 9,478			$ 54			$ 54			$ 54	$ 9,639
Total Expenses			$ 9,478			$ 91			$ 204			$ 86	$ 9,859

CUSTOMERS

What do customers value? Customer satisfaction depends on many factors, but the old stalwarts are low prices, good quality, and responsiveness to their needs. For the purposes of our analysis, let's focus on the speed of response to a customer inquiry for service. This response time is driven by the duration of all of the tasks between the submittal of a lead to the delivery of services in accordance with the customer needs.

Which specific tasks within our process models are involved in this value stream? The tasks cited in **Figure 32** are a good place to start. All of these tasks except one reside in the Steve's Sales process model. The other task resides in Debra's Service Delivery process model. This demonstrates a very powerful feature of value streams. They can be used to analyze dependencies between functions in your organization.

Figure 32 Customer Value Stream

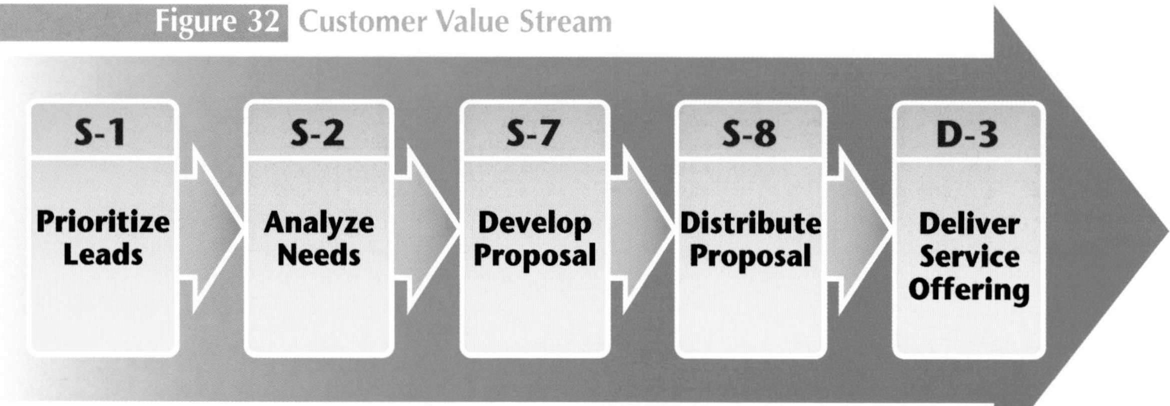

The key to improving response time is to avoid re-inventing the wheel for every task in **Figure 32.** Steve currently uses a sheet of loose-leaf paper daily to create a prioritized list of leads requiring his attention for the day. His assessment of each lead is based upon his knowledge of the respective client or hunches based upon the source of the lead. When he is uncomfortable with his hunches, he will take the time to call the client and perhaps even schedule a meeting to better assess their needs. Steve develops each proposal from scratch, and once he finishes, his assistant sends the proposal to the client via postal mail. Once the client accepts the proposal, the pertinent member of Debra's staff delivers the contract in accordance with their individual best practices. The time it takes to deliver a given service can vary significantly between staff members.

Table 11 / Customer Value Stream Metrics

Task ID	S-1			S-2			S-7			S-8			D-3			
Task Description	**Prioritize Leads**			**Analyze Leads**			**Develop Proposal**			**Distribute Proposal**			**Deliver Service Offering**			TOTALS
Timing																
Task Duration	0.25		hrs	1		hrs	8		hrs	0.5		hrs	160		hrs	170
Handoff Lag Time	0		hrs	0		hrs	16		hrs	168		hrs	0		hrs	184
Total Time	0.25		hrs	1		hrs	24		hrs	168.5		hrs	160		hrs	354
Quality																
% On-Time Start	50%			100%			50%			50%			50%			6%
% On-Time Finish	50%			100%			50%			50%			50%			6%
Expenses																
Labor Expenses	*# Heads*		*Rate*	*# Heads*		*Rate*		*# Heads*	*Rate*		*# Heads*	*Rate*		*# Heads*	*Rate*	
Senior Staff	1		$ 150	1		$ 150	1		$ 150	1		$ 150	1		$ 150	
Administrative Support	0		$ 50	0		$ 50	0		$ 50	0.25		$ 50	0.25		$ 50	
Labor Subtotal			*$ 38*			*$ 150*			*$ 1,200*			*$ 81*			*$ 26,000*	*$ 27,469*
Technology	*Deploy*	*Ops*	*% Alloc*	*Deploy*	*Ops*	*% Alloc*	*Deploy*	*Ops*	*% Alloc*	*Deploy*	*Ops*	*% Alloc*	*Deploy*	*Ops*	*% Alloc*	
Windows XP	$2,240	$3,119	0.01	$ 2,240	$3,119	0.01	$2,240	$ 3,119	0.01	$2,240	$3,119	0.01	$2,240	$ 3,119	0.01	
MS Office	$ 440	$3,083	0.01	$ 440	$3,083	0.01	$ 440	$ 3,083	0.01	$ 440	$3,083	0.01	$ 440	$ 3,083	0.01	
Technology Subtotal			*$ 54*			*$ 54*			*$ 54*			*$ 54*			*$ 54*	*$ 268*
Total Expenses			*$ 91*			*$ 204*			*$ 1,254*			*$ 135*			*$ 26,054*	*$ 27,737*

Where are the value stream improvement opportunities amidst the data presented in **Table 11**? We could reduce the time it takes Steve to prioritize leads from 0.25 hrs to 0 hrs if all the leads, independent of their source, were merged automatically into a single report for Steve. The leads in the report could be automatically prioritized by adding values for a few standard fields when the lead is entered (e.g. revenue opportunity, customer rating, likelihood of purchase). Steve's proposal development time could be reduced from 8 hrs to less than 1 hr if the majority of proposals could be automatically created from the information captured in the lead and the latest service offering data. Proposals could be automatically queued for distribution to clients by deploying a document workflow automation system. Proposal distribution time could be ▶

Table 12 / Customer Value Stream Opportunities

Task ID	S-1			S-2			S-7			S-8			D-3			
Task Description	**Prioritize Leads**			**Analyze Leads**			**Develop Proposal**			**Distribute Proposal**			**Deliver Service Offering**			TOTALS
Timing																
Task Duration	0		hrs	1		hrs	1		hrs	0.25		hrs	0		hrs	2
Handoff Lag Time	0		hrs	0		hrs	0		hrs	0		hrs	0		hrs	0
Total Time		0	hrs		1	hrs		1	hrs		0.25	hrs		0	hrs	2
Quality																
% On-Time Start			50%			100%			50%			50%			50%	6%
% On-Time Finish			50%			100%			50%			50%			50%	6%
Expenses																
Labor Expenses	# Heads		Rate	# Heads		Rate		# Heads	Rate		# Heads	Rate		# Heads	Rate	
Senior Staff		0	$ 150		1	$ 150		1	$ 150		0.1	$ 150		0	$ 150	
Administrative Support		0	$ 50		0	$ 50		0	$ 50		1	$ 50		0	$ 50	
Labor Subtotal			$ -			$ 150			$ 150			$ 16			$ -	$ 316
Technology	Deploy	Ops	% Alloc	Deploy	Ops	% Alloc	Deploy	Ops	% Alloc	Deploy	Ops	% Alloc	Deploy	Ops	% Alloc	
Windows XP				$2,240	$3,119	0.01	$2,240	$3,119	0.01	$2,240	$3,119	0.01	$2,240	$ 3,119	0.01	
MS Office				$ 440	$3,083	0.01	$ 440	$3,083	0.01	$ 440	$3,083	0.01	$ 440	$ 3,083	0.01	
Technology Subtotal			$ -			$ 54			$ 54			$ 54			$ 54	$ 214
Total Expenses			$ -			$ 204			$ 204			$ 70			$ 54	$ 531

reduced from a week to minutes if clients would accept electronic submissions.

As cited earlier, Debra's Service Delivery load could be lightened by packaging some service offerings for on-demand access by clients via the web. These opportunities have been highlighted in **Table 12**. All of these opportunities indicate a promising outlook for the improvement of customer responsiveness – not to mention more time for the Sales team to generate sales.

EMPLOYEES

What do Employees value? Employee needs are diverse, but one item stands out. The work week for salaried personnel at Professional Service Firms is typically much longer than the standard 40-hour work week. These hours are driven by the persistent push for billable hours coupled with attractive performance-based compensation packages for workaholic drive. Few things are more annoying to employees working long hours than the need to spend time on activities that distract them from achieving their performance goals or simply spending quality time with their family.

In this spirit, let's focus on non-billable activities such as timekeeping, expense tracking, and training as cited in **Figure 33.** All of these tasks reside in the Service Delivery process model.

Figure 33 Employee Value Stream

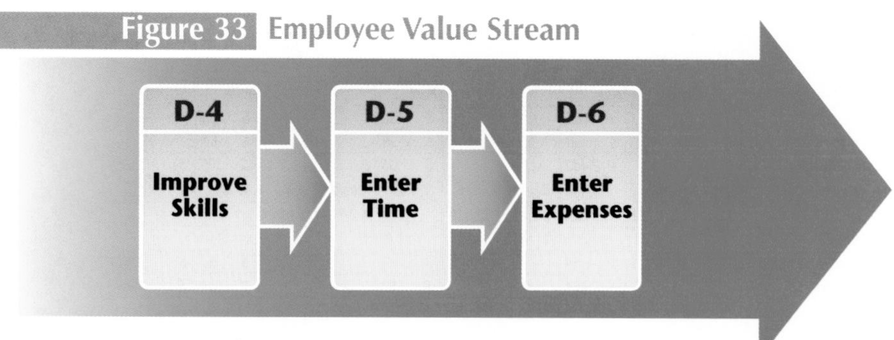

There are several keys to improving the performance of this value stream from the perspective of your employees. Debra and her team spend a lot of time on the road working with clients and often are unable to attend training sessions at the home office. A way to offer training to employees that worked around their schedules would better ensure their participation. Another concern for Debra and her team is the cumbersome task of making copies of expense receipts and forwarding them to folks in Finance. A way to simplify the entry of time and expense information would be a welcomed development.

Table 13 / Employee Value Stream Metrics

Task ID	D-4			D-5			D-6			TOTALS
Task Description	**Improve Skills**			**Enter Time**			**Enter Expenses**			
Timing										
Task Duration	16		hrs	0.25		hrs	2		hrs	18
Handoff Lag Time	0		hrs	0		hrs	0		hrs	0
Total Time	16		hrs	0.25		hrs	2		hrs	18
Quality										
% On-Time Start	20%			100%			100%			20%
% On-Time Finish	100%			100%			100%			100%
Expenses										
Labor Expenses	*# Heads*		*Rate*	*# Heads*		*Rate*		*# Heads*	*Rate*	
Senior Staff	1		$ 150	1		$ 150	1		$ 150	
Administrative Support	0		$ 50	0		$ 50	0		$ 50	
Labor Subtotal			*$ 2,400*			*$ 38*			*$ 300*	*$ 2,738*
Technology	*Deploy*	*Ops*	*% Alloc*	*Deploy*	*Ops*	*% Alloc*	*Deploy*	*Ops*	*% Alloc*	
Windows XP	$2,240	$3,119	0.01	$ 2,240	$3,119	0.01	$2,240	$3,119	0.01	
MS Office				$ 440	$3,083	0.01	$ 440	$3,083	0.01	
Technology Subtotal			*$ 54*			*$ 54*			*$ 54*	*$ 161*
Total Expenses			*$ 2,454*			*$ 91*			*$ 354*	*$ 2,898*

Where are the value stream improvement opportunities amidst the values presented in **Table 13**? If we were to migrate the majority of these training courses to a web-based delivery format, employees could access training whenever and from wherever they are available. This would increase the likelihood that employees could start training at their leisure, and, more importantly, finish it as well. Once you eliminate coffee breaks, travel time, introductions, and Q&A tangents from the training equation, you might also be able to reduce the training time required. As cited earlier, we could reduce the time it takes to enter expenses if they were tracked by a credit card provider with smart tracking services. These opportunities have been highlighted in **Table 14.** This is but a small sample of options available to improve employee satisfaction. The important concept to remember is that it is much easier to identify and quantify opportunities within a quantitative framework such as that presented in our value stream metrics tables.

Table 14 / Employee Value Stream Opportunities

Task ID	D-4			D-5			D-6			TOTALS
Task Description	**Improve Skills**			**Enter Time**			**Enter Expenses**			
Timing										
Task Duration	2		hrs	0.25		hrs	1		hrs	3
Handoff Lag Time	0		hrs	0		hrs	0		hrs	0
Total Time	2		hrs	0.25		hrs	1		hrs	3
Quality										
% On-Time Start	100%			100%			100%			100%
% On-Time Finish	100%			100%			100%			100%
Expenses										
Labor Expenses	*# Heads*		*Rate*	*# Heads*		*Rate*		*# Heads*	*Rate*	
Senior Staff	1		$ 150	1		$ 150	1		$ 150	
Administrative Support	0		$ 50	0		$ 50	0		$ 50	
Labor Subtotal			*$ 300*			*$ 38*			*$ 150*	*$ 488*
Technology	*Deploy*	*Ops*	*% Alloc*	*Deploy*	*Ops*	*% Alloc*	*Deploy*	*Ops*	*% Alloc*	
Windows XP	$2,240	$3,119	0.01	$ 2,240	$ 3,119	0.01	$ 2,240	$ 3,119	0.01	
MS Office				$ 440	$ 3,083	0.01	$ 440	$ 3,083	0.01	
Technology Subtotal			*$ 54*			*$ 54*			*$ 54*	*$ 161*
Total Expenses			*$ 354*			*$ 91*			*$ 204*	*$ 648*

Objectives

Our value stream assessments have revealed several significant opportunities for improving our business performance. **Table 15** provides us with a summary of these opportunities. The potential performance values resulting from these opportunities can now be converted into performance objectives. By recasting our business model into concise value streams, we have reason to believe that these objectives are realistic. More than realistic, these objectives have been defined in such a way as to create lasting change within our organization, unlike a shotgun objective such as cutting expenses across the board by 10%. Each value stream features a set of tasks that are repeated as part of normal operations. A tangible scenario formed the basis of our performance improvement opportunities for each task. The actual implementation of these scenarios will be addressed in **Step 5.**

Table 15 / Value Stream Improvement Opportunities

Value Stream	Current Performance				Potential Performance				% Improvement			
	Duration(hrs)	Cost ($)	Quality		Duration(hrs)	Cost ($)	Quality		Duration	Cost	Quality	
			Start	Finish			Start	Finish			Start	Finish
Stakeholders	163	26633	25%	25%	2	9859	25%	25%	99%	63%	0%	0%
Customers	354	27737	6%	6%	2	584	6%	6%	99%	98%	0%	0%
Employees	18	2896	20%	100%	3	648	100%	100%	83%	78%	400%	0%

While understanding the opportunities to improve our value streams is important, we would also like to be able generate scorecards for each of our functional managers. In order to create these scorecards, we need to look at all of the tasks in the functional process model and adjust the metrics for tasks that can be improved per our value stream analysis. This means that you will need to apply the worksheets that we used for value stream tasks to each task in your process model. For example, the results of this exercise for the Service Delivery function would look something like **Table 16.** If we make a simplifying assumption that each task is executed once per review period, this exercise would provide you with tangible performance benchmarks for your functional departments and your overall business. It will take much more effort to complete than simply focusing on a few value streams, but it will provide you with solid cost and revenue benchmarks for each ▶

Table 16 / Service Delivery Process Improvement Opportunities

ID	Task	Current Performance				Potential Performance				% Improvement			
		Duration (hrs)	Cost ($)	Quality		Duration (hrs)	Cost ($)	Quality		Duration	Cost	Quality	
				Start	Finish			Start	Finish			Start	Finish
D-1	Develop Service Offering	160	16000	25%	25%	160	16000	25%	25%	0%	0%	0%	0%
D-2	Train Personnel	40	4000	25%	25%	40	4000	25%	25%	0%	0%	0%	0%
D-3	Deliver Service Offering	160	26054	50%	50%	0	648	100%	100%	100%	98%	100%	100%
D-4	Improve Skills	163	26633	20%	100%	2	434	100%	100%	99%	98%	400%	0%
D-5	Enter Time	354	27737	100%	100%	2	584	100%	100%	99%	98%	0%	0%
D-6	Enter Expenses	18	2896	100%	100%	3	648	100%	100%	83%	78%	0%	0%
D-7	Prepare Staff Requisition	1	100	75%	100%	1	100	75%	100%	0%	0%	0%	0%
D-8	Define Personnel Objectives	8	800	75%	75%	8	800	75%	75%	0%	0%	0%	0%
D-9	Evaluate Personnel	16	1600	20%	50%	16	1600	20%	50%	0%	0%	0%	0%
D-10	Prepare Case Study	16	1600	25%	50%	16	1600	25%	50%	0%	0%	0%	0%
D-11	Distribute Leads	1	100	50%	50%	1	100	50%	50%	0%	0%	0%	0%
D-12	Generate Status Report	8	800	70%	80%	8	800	70%	80%	0%	0%	0%	0%
D-13	Monitor Performance	160	16000	50%	50%	160	16000	50%	50%	0%	0%	0%	0%
	TOTAL	1105	124320	53%	66%	417	43314	63%	70%	62%	65%	19%	6%

organization. Once these benchmarks have been established, you will only have to use the simplified value stream approach going forward.

The gathering of all of this information is part of the "aiming" process. While this can be labor intensive, clearly it is not as labor intensive as it would be if you were to analyze each and every task in the processes that form our overall business model. Improving your business performance costs money. The old adage "you need to spend money to make money" rings true whether or not computers are involved. It is advised that you postpone a comprehensive analysis until you have implemented IT systems that specifically address business process management and business performance management. Our goal is to ensure that your business improvement funds generate a healthy return on investment. Ultimately, this will be captured on our business scorecard in the form of increased sales, lower expenses and increased profit margins.

Step 4 Review

We have covered a lot of ground so far with our IT Roadmap. In **Step 1** we took a high-level view of Professional Service Firm operations that allowed us to evaluate our Strengths, Weaknesses, Opportunities and Threats relative to other business models. In **Step 2,** we went beyond this high-level view and identified individual tasks that represent our daily activities. In **Step 3,** we provided methods for us to analyze the costs and revenue associated with these activities. We also showed how we could capture these metrics in a scorecard. Upon completing **Step 4,** we now have a method for defining objectives that we can use to guide decisions about where to invest our resources. Now, how do we achieve these objectives? This question will be answered in the next section.

You have now passed by the following IT Roadmap milestones:

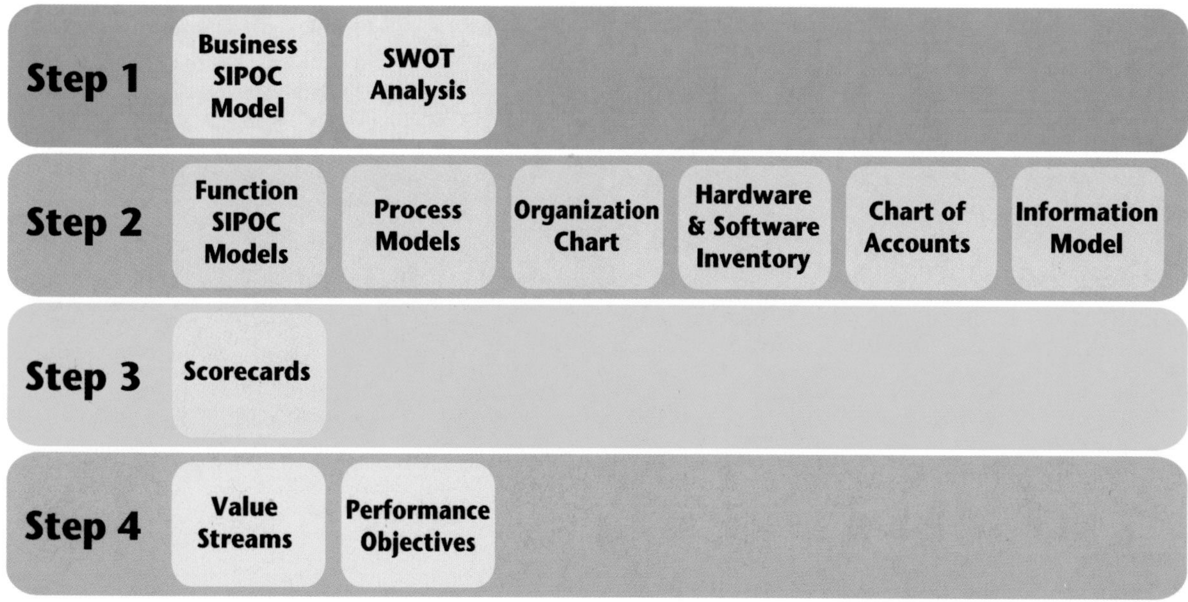

STEP 5: HOW ARE YOU GOING TO GET YOUR BUSINESS THERE?

"Bold objectives require conservative engineering".

James E. Webb, second NASA Administrator / *Space Age Management, The Large-Scale Approach* (McGraw Hill, 1969)

OK...you know where you are. You know where you want to go. Now you need to know "how do I get there?" This section is all about building bridges. While we are not talking about bridges between the Earth and the Moon, we do want to build bridges between the current performance of your business and the bold objectives you have for your business.

Your value stream assessments revealed a few gaps between where your business is today and where you would like to be. On the advice of Mr. Webb above, this section will outline a "conservative" approach to filling these gaps designed to minimize the risk of a failed deployment followed by buyer's remorse. This approach features three basic steps:

- Define a strategy for how you plan to fill the gaps.
- Execute your strategy using project management best practices.
- Track that status of your execution.

Several common, but generally unsuccessful, alternatives to this approach are summarized in **Table 17.** The pitfalls of these approaches can be summed up in one observation:

Technology is driving your business, not the other way around!

Ian the IT Manager for Superior Services was ready to get under the hood of the company's IT Roadmap. He had spent the past few weeks documenting the business processes for the other functions, understanding what resources supported each process, and analyzing the opportunities for improving each process. The next challenge that he faced was how to take advantage of these opportunities. Ian's IT organization was not large. It consisted of Ian and a jack-▶

of-all-trades assistant to help with system backups and configuring laptops. Before tempting the other managers with a smorgasbord of IT products and services that he might struggle to deliver with his current staff, he first needed to define a strategy.

Table 17 / Alternative Gap-Filling Approaches

Approach	Description	Appeal	Pitfalls
Shiny objects	Impulse buying in response to marketing ad or demo.	Immediate gratification.	Advanced software solutions take time to configure.
			May not interact well with other software applications.
Keeping up with the Jones'	A competitor uses a given technology so you decide to use it.	Appears to be low risk.	What works for them and their business model, may not work for you.
		Neutralizes any competitive advantage that competitor may have.	Loss of IT as a possible differentiator between you and your competition.
Trial and error	Purchase first product with the features you think that you need. If it doesn't work out, move on to the next vendor.	Avoids analysis paralysis.	May require expensive mid-stream changes.
			Ineffective use of resources and disrupts core operations.

Strategy

Defining your IT strategy is simple in concept. We have defined where we currently are as a business in regards to performance. We have defined where we want to be in regard to performance. Now all we need to do is fill the gap in between where we are and where we want to be. Gaps are problems. These problems can be resolved in a variety of ways. We will refer to these "ways" as "solutions".

Figure 34 Gap Assessment

SOLUTIONS

A "Solution" is one of those buzz-words that IT natives like to use. The "What Ifs" that accompanied our SWOT Analysis in Step 1 referred to some IT solutions. We also alluded to some solutions in context of our value stream assessments in Step 4. Solutions can feature staffing (i.e. People), process services, technology or any combination thereof. Professional Service Firms should be very comfortable with the notion of service-based solutions in particular. That's what you do. For example, the service offerings for an accounting firm would be tax or audit services while the service offerings of a legal firm would be brief filing or consultation. Technology solutions can be as simple as installing Microsoft Office on a single desktop PC or as complex as an Enterprise Resource Planning system deployed to hundreds of users on a client-server network. One of the goals of the IT Roadmap is to introduce you to software solutions that have typically only been employed by businesses with a large number of IT specialists on staff. More often than not, the performance benefits of these solutions apply to both small and large businesses. It has become increasingly easier for business users with limited IT knowledge to configure advanced solutions that build upon the basic capabilities of the ubiquitous Windows XP and Microsoft Office.

Ian had come across the term "solution" many times in his IT professional journals, but he had never given it much thought. He was typically focused on how to fight the latest virus threat or tips and tricks on improving the performance of their email server. The challenge of putting together an IT Roadmap made him pause at, rather than fly by, the word "solution". It turns out that he had only been scratching the surface of IT opportunities with the company's email server and website. He now found himself signing up for free webinars and blogs that introduced him to a world of new possibilities.

PROFILES

An important reason we spent time breaking your business down into core functions was to make it easier to identify which solutions might best be able to help you **(See Figure 35).** Along with this knowledge, understanding the language of IT solution providers is key, given the thousands of technology offerings currently on the market (and this number is growing daily). As a start, **Table 18** lists the basic "sorting bins" IT providers use to categorize their solutions. A small sample of these solutions is summarized in **Appendix 1** along with contact information for solution providers that will help you implement these solutions.

Table 18 / Solution Types

Solution Type	Description
Infrastructure	Provides services typically not of any concern to end users, such as operating systems and database management software.
Collaboration	Enhances ability to share information between users.
Customer Relationship Management	Provides ability to track most aspects of the touchpoints between a business and its customers.
Financials	Provides general ledger, accounts payable, and accounts receivable functions, including time and expense management.
Business Process Management	Provides the ability to define and manage workflows pertinent to your daily business operations.
Business Performance Measurement	Provides senior management with the ability to track the status of key performance indicators across the business.
Enterprise Project Management	Provides a centralized repository of project information that can be used to track resource assignments, standardize project management methods, or provide project status.

Figure 35 Solution-Process Relationships

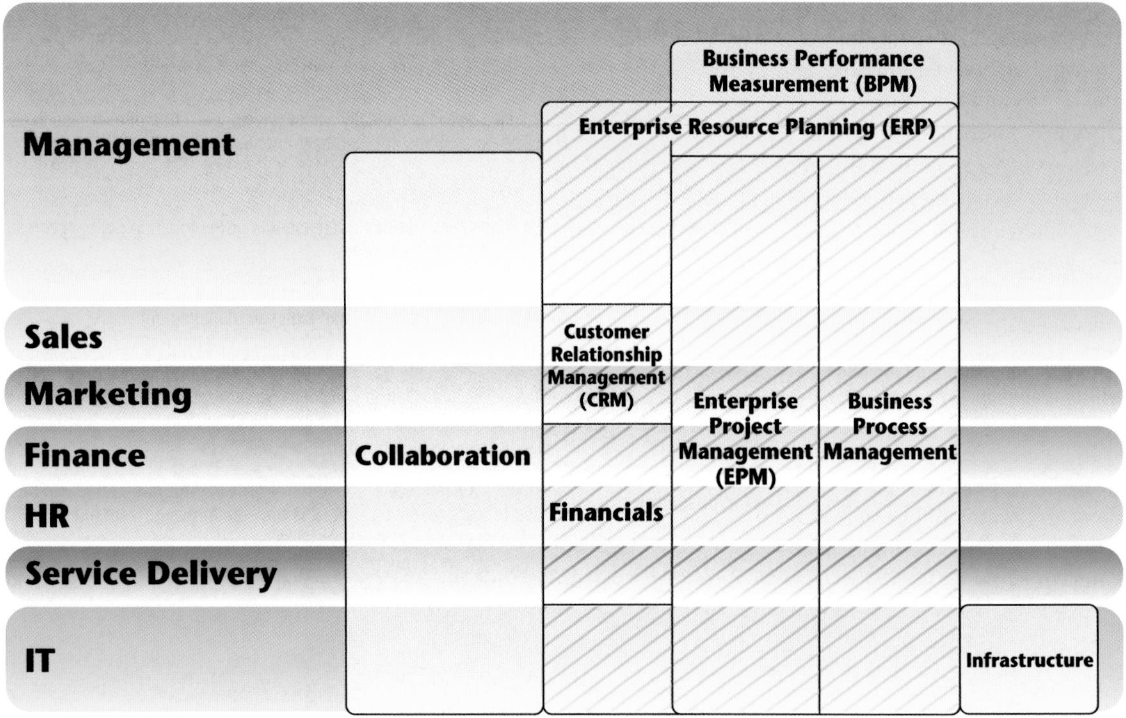

Solutions can span multiple functional organizations or be focused on a single functional area. How many functional areas a solution includes is often referred to as the "horizontal" scope. In addition to this horizontal scope, many solutions also have what is called a "vertical" scope. The vertical scope refers to the industry or industries in which a solution is used. One way of characterizing the horizontal and vertical scope of solutions is shown in **Figure 36**. While the Standard Industrial Classification (SIC) code can be a useful reference in understanding how some businesses view industry verticals, most software companies take quite a bit of liberty with their definition of verticals. In addition to this variance, the scope of verticals can vary quite a bit in granularity.

For example, the Professional Service Firms vertical can be further refined into a Law Firms vertical. You may have noticed that this book is targeted at all horizontal functions within the Professional Services vertical. If this observation came to mind, you are well on your way towards speaking "IT". If it didn't come to mind, don't worry, you can always bring your dictionary with you when you visit with the IT natives.

Figure 36 Horizontal vs Vertical Scope

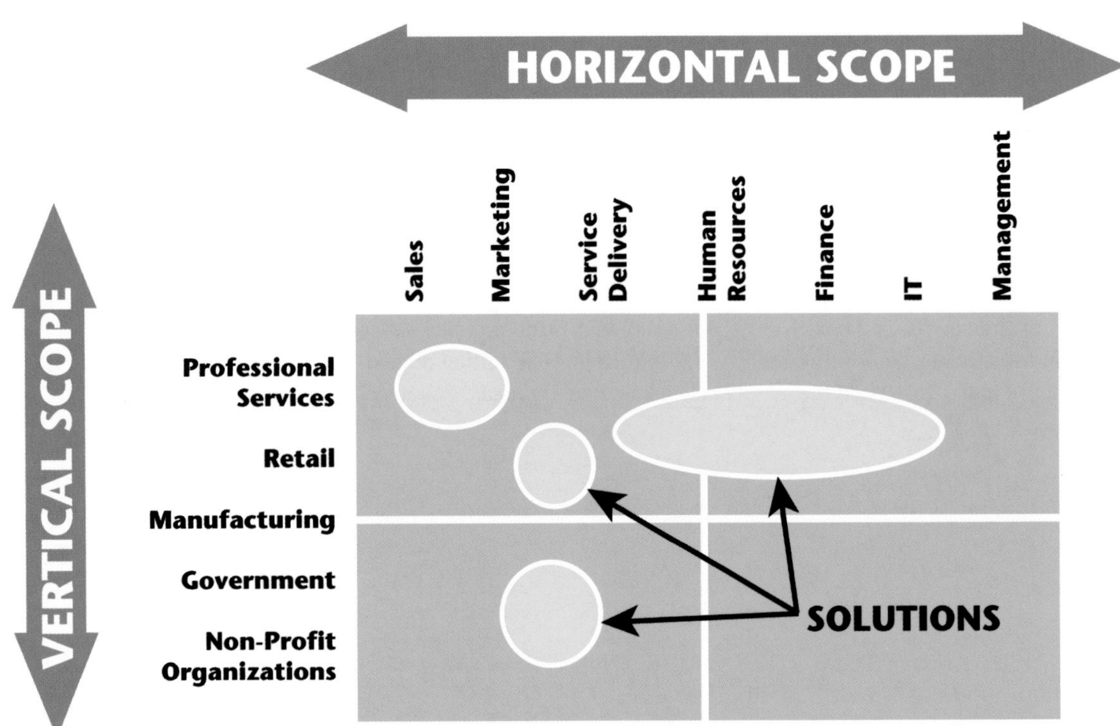

The sheer number of IT solution options facing Ian was a bit overwhelming. By understanding that solutions could be grouped by business process helped make it more manageable. By understanding how the IT industry uses "horizontals" and "verticals" to further structure these solutions, Ian was able to conduct more effective searches for information on solutions that appeared to support the needs of Superior Services. His research on solutions also prompted him to consider what type of IT organization would be required to support the deployment and support of these solutions. Now it is time to identify some specific solutions to close our performance gaps.

Appendix 1 profiles a small sample of the solutions available. Each solution profile contains the following information:

- Description of features
- Benefits in context of our value streams
- Solution dependencies
- Deployment costs (labor plus technology)
- Operating costs (labor plus technology)
- Where to go for additional information

These solution profiles are excellent starting points for your exploration of the world of advanced IT solutions. Companies that specialize in providing solutions for small business have provided many of these profiles.

PLANNING

Strategic planning can take many forms. For our purposes, let's keep it simple: no dates – no costs. Let's just focus on identifying the right steps in our IT Roadmap. We'll figure out how big those steps are and how much they cost in the next section.

Let's start out by examining the size of our gaps. These gaps were organized in **Table 15** by value streams. Each of the solution profiles has been evaluated to determine the potential impact of the solution upon each value stream. The results of these evaluations can be found in **Table 19.** Let's focus our strategic planning first on the Stakeholder value stream for Superior Services. **Table 19** summarizes the projected impacts of each of our solutions upon the Stakeholder value stream. From this table, we notice that INF-3 offers significant benefits to the Stakeholder values stream. INF-3 matches up to the Microsoft Small Business Server Standard Edition which includes advanced security, collaboration, administration, and mobility features that will help improve office productivity. Upon closer examination of the solution profile in **Appendix 1,** we note several solution dependencies ▶

Table 19 / Solution Impact Summary

ID	Title	Customer Benefit Summary	Employee Benefit Summary	Stakeholder Benefit Summary	Complexity	Expense
Business Performance Measurement						
BPM-1	Business Scorecard Manager	Medium	Medium	High	Medium	Medium
Business Process Management						
PRO-1	AgilePoint	Medium	Medium	High	Medium	High
PRO-2	BizTalk	Medium	NA	High	High	High
Collaboration						
COM-1	MS Office Small Business Edition	Medium	Medium	High	Low	Low
COM-2	Live Meeting	Medium	Medium	High	Low	Low
Customer Relationship Management						
CRM-1	Results Business Suite	High	Low	Medium	Medium	Medium
CRM-2	Microsoft Dynamics™ CRM	High	Low	Medium	Medium	Medium
CRM-3	Microsoft Dynamics™ CRM Live	High	Low	Medium	Low	Medium
Enterprise Project Management						
EPM-1	Microsoft Office Project	Medium	Low	Medium	Low	Low
EPM-2	Project Server	Medium	Medium	High	High	Medium
Financial Management						
FIN-1	Small Business Accounting	Low	Medium	Medium	Low	Low
FIN-2	Small Business Financials	Medium	Medium	High	High	High
Infrastructure						
INF-1	Windows XP	NA	Low	Medium	Low	Low
INF-2	Windows Server	Low	Medium	Medium	Medium	Medium
INF-3	Small Business Server	Low	High	High	Medium	Medium
INF-4	SQL Server	NA	Low	Medium	Medium	Low

Impact assessments are based upon the value streams identified in this book. Results may vary for the value streams specific to your business. Contact a Microsoft Partner near you for an assessment specific to your business needs (See Solution Builder in ***Appendix 3****).*

Figure 37 Gap-Filling Strategy

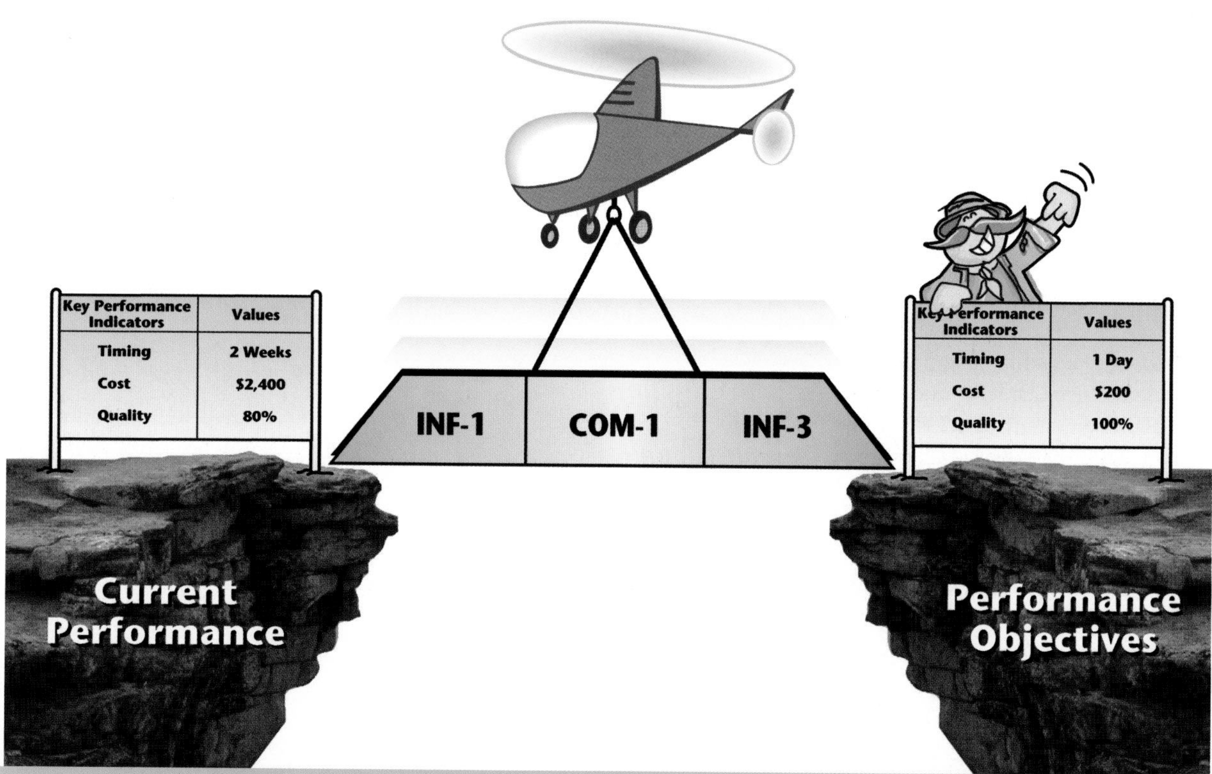

that need to be addressed. In order to deploy INF-3 solution, we find from the INF-3 solution profile in **Appendix 1** that the INF-3 solution is dependent upon INF-1 and COM-1. In order to deploy COM-1, INF-1 is necessary. A logical sequence for the deployment of the solutions is now starting to take shape. INF-1 pertains to the installation of Windows XP on all client machines (i.e. desktops and laptops). Luckily, INF-1 is already in place for most of the workforce. Ian will need to upgrade the remaining computers intended to use COM-1 to the Windows XP operating system. Once this has been done, he can deploy all of the COM-1 features to these computers. Now Ian is ready to deploy INF-3. **Figure 37** summarizes the sequence in which the performance gap might be filled. We could take a similar approach to the creation of a gap-fill strategy for our Customer and Employee value streams.

IT ORGANIZATION

The solutions you need to employ to fill your performance gaps will drive what type of IT organization you will need to fill these gaps and keep them filled. Underpinning your IT strategy is a fundamental decision: what kind of IT organization do you want to have? Do you want IT skills to be a core competency for your business or do you prefer to contract with other businesses to provide your company with IT resources? The spectrum of options available in this regard is summarized in **Figure 38.** Each option involves pro's and con's. Additionally, you may very well choose to morph into different types of IT organizations over the course of time.

Figure 38 IT Organization Types

	Basic	Infrastructure	Development
Feature	• Informal IT "guru" in office • Peer-to-Peer network • Website hosted by 3rd Party • Advanced software solutions hosted by 3rd Party if necessary	• Dedicated IT support staff • Client-Server network • Public Website internally hosted • Private Website (Intranet) internally hosted • Advanced software solutions hosted internally • 3rd parties provide any custom solutions that might be required	• Dedicated staff of software developers • Development and test environments • Dedicated IT support staff • Client-Server network • Website internally hosted • Advanced software solutions hosted internally
Pros	• Minimal IT knowledge required • Minimal IT investment required	• Accountability for IT support performance • Ability to scale as company grows • Decreased risk of poor IT deployments • Access to significant number of performance improvement solutions	• Ability to supplement service offerings with product offerings that enhance services • Increased flexibility in the number of performance improvement solution options available • Accountability for overall IT performance
Cons	• Difficult to scale as company grows • Information critical to business and potentially to clients hosted by 3rd party • Minimal performance improvement options • Riskier deployments of IT solutions	• Must continually invest in IT administration skills development • Must continually invest in IT infrastructure • Difficult to leverage IT as a competitive differentiator	• Must continuously invest in IT programming skills development • Must continually invest in IT administration skills • Must continually invest in IT infrastructure

Now, let's see how to put this strategy to some practical use.

Execution

Having a strategy is important, but execution is critical. In this section, we will go over recommended best practices for converting strategy to execution. In the strategy section above, we deliberately kept cost and timing out of the picture in order to simplify matters. However, in order to execute our strategy effectively, we now need to bring them back into the frame along with another important aspect of execution – scope.

SCOPE

The question "What is the scope of your work?" is the management equivalent to the 20 Question staple "Is it bigger than a breadbox?" In order to be executed effectively, work needs to be broken up into bite-size chunks of activities that are easier to manage. **Steps 1** and **2** guided us through a successive refinement of the scope of our business operations. We started off in **Figure 5** with a very high-level view of the overall business. In **Figure 6** we broke down the operations of the business into functional departments and later developed SIPOC models to describe how these functional departments exchange information. In our process models, we further refined the scope of our discussions to address individual tasks within each functional organization. We will distill our scope even further in this section, but the topic will not be our daily operations. Instead, this section will focus on those activities designed to change these operations in a manner that will help us meet our performance objectives. These agents of change will be referred to as programs and projects.

Project Manager

A good project manager is much more than a manager who has been assigned to a project.
Project Management is a unique discipline like accounting or engineering.
Project management professional societies such as the Project Management Institute (**www.pmi.org**) have defined standards against which project management practioners can be certified in a manner similar to that used for CPAs.

In the same way our business model features a group of process models, a program is a group of projects. A unique program will be established for each value stream and a unique project for each deployment of a solution. The gap-filling strategy for each value stream will then help define our list of projects for each program. For example, the Superior Services Stakeholder Program would feature a preliminary list of the following projects: INF-1, COM-1, and INF-3.

It should be emphasized that a solution does not necessarily equate to a project. While this may be the case for simple solutions, not all solutions are simple – especially the solutions that tend to provide the greatest benefit to your organization. Before deploying a complex solution to everyone in your business, ask the solution vendor to develop a "proof of concept" first. If the proof of concept appears to address your business needs, proceed on to pilot deployment of the solution to a select number of users who would best be able to gauge the impact of the solution on business operations. If the solution passes muster with the pilot group, then you can deploy it throughout your business with a high degree of confidence. Medium complexity projects might only need a pilot deployment project prior to rolling the system out to all users, while low complexity projects can often be deployed straight to production (i.e. all users). Along the way, you will have minimized your financial risk and risk to your daily operations.

Project Supports Multiple Programs

When you identify which solutions are necessary to fill the gaps of multiple programs, you may find some overlap between the solutions required by the different value streams. This is good. It means that by deploying a solution to meet one set of performance objectives, it actually supports meeting another set of performance objectives. You need to make sure that you don't spend limited resources deploying the same solution more than once, though. Dependencies such as this should be noted in your program documentation.

Table 20 / Deployment Project Types

Project Type	Solution Complexity	Why?
Proof of Concept	High	Demonstrate ability of solution to satisfy business needs with minimal risk.
Pilot	Medium, High	Validate ability of solution to improve business operations with subset of users.
Production	Low, Medium, High	Implement solution to improve business operations.

Each type of deployment corresponds to a project type. The different solution project types are summarized in **Table 20.** **Table 19** includes an assessment deployment risk for each solution. Each of the solutions identified to fill the gaps for the Stakeholder Value Stream in **Figure 37** have a low deployment complexity with the exception of INF-3, which is rated as medium complexity. The scope of the Stakeholder program, as reflected in its project list, would therefore be modified slightly to address multiple deployment projects for INF-3 to manage the complexity. The INF-3 production project would be supplemented by an INF-3 Pilot deployment project.

Virtual Servers

Virtual Server software provides one avenue for replicating your solution in multiple environments without the need to purchase additional hardware.
This approach is not without its impacts.
It typically takes a significant portion of the host server's memory to run multiple virtual servers which can adversely impact the performance for all instances of the solution.

The scope of the projects within a program is driven by many considerations:

- Number of requirements
- Number of system components
- Number of system interfaces
- Deployment audience

The first three considerations correspond to the hidden complexity alluded to beneath the waterline in **Figure 3.** The last consideration, deployment audience, is related to the deployment project type. The collection of components that appear below the waterline in **Figure 3** is often referred to as an environment. Many projects require multiple instances or copies of each solution in order to meet the needs of multiple project team activities. A summary of the typical environments and their associated purposes is provided in **Table 21.** Be sure to ask your solution provider if they will be creating multiple solution environments. If they have no plans to do so, be sure that you are comfortable with the risks that are raised by not creating them.

Table 21 / Solution Environments

Environment	Purpose	Risks if not used
Development	Provide an environment wherein the solution configuration can evolve and be tested prior to rolling the solution to production.	Random system outages and configuration changes commonly present during development may create a first impression on end users that is not very favorable.
Demonstration	Provide a stable, persistent environment suitable for demonstrations.	Solution configuration may change from known configuration prior to demonstrating system to broader audiences (e.g. customers, senior management). Surprises such as this tend to impact presentation quality and the perception of the solution by the demonstration audience.
Training	Provide an environment that supports scripted training exercises.	Configuration changes may lead to differences with content of training materials and subsequent confusion for trainees. Unable to reset configuration after each training session to ensure consistency of environment for each class.
Production	Provide a stable environment for end users.	End users may be confused or distracted by major system configuration changes. Data in system may be corrupted as a result of these changes.

All of these scope considerations translate into the labor effort required for projects and their parent programs. Recalling **Equation 2** in **Step 3,** effort is tied to the number of people assigned to a task (your connection to labor expenses) and the duration of the task. This link is the key to keeping the assumptions that you have around the scope of your programs and projects consistent with your timing and cost assumptions.

TIMING

How long will it take to deploy the solutions you need to fill your value stream gaps? A reasonable answer to that question is "it depends". The time it takes to complete a program or project depends primarily upon the effort required and the budget available. In deference to this response, many programs and projects start out with an end date before the scope or cost is known. If your organization has significant experience deploying similar solutions, this approach does not add a huge amount of risk to your programs or projects. However, if this is not the case, it is strongly recommended that you go through a few planning iterations including considerations of all the programs and projects on your plate before nailing down a time constraint if possible.

As we look at what it takes to execute our strategy, it is impractical to deploy all of the projects within a program at the same time. Several appetite suppressants exist for small businesses eager to bite off more than they can chew at once. Cash flow is probably the most common. Most small businesses do not have a large stash of cash sitting on the sidelines waiting for a technology solution to ride in on a white horse. If by some chance you do happen to have such a stash, there is a more subtle throttling mechanism that you should consider: your staff. Your staff needs to support the core operations of your company while the solution is being deployed. They also are the source of requirements for the new solutions as well as the folks responsible for testing the new system to make sure that it meets these requirements. If executed improperly, a program can quickly overwhelm the capacity of your staff. So, in order to address these concerns, we need to space out the timing of your programs and projects.

How much time a program will take is simply a roll-up of the time it takes to execute its projects. How much time it takes to execute a project is simply a roll-up of the time it takes to execute the tasks necessary to complete the project. Projects are very similar to processes in this respect. The duration of individual tasks is simply a function of the effort required to complete a task and the number of resources assigned to the task. If you assume that one staff member works on a set of activities requiring 40 person-hours, then it would take 40 hours to complete the task which typically correlates to one week. If two staff members work together on the same task, that task should be completed within two and a half days, and so on. The good news is that sev- ▶

Figure 39 Sample Program Plan

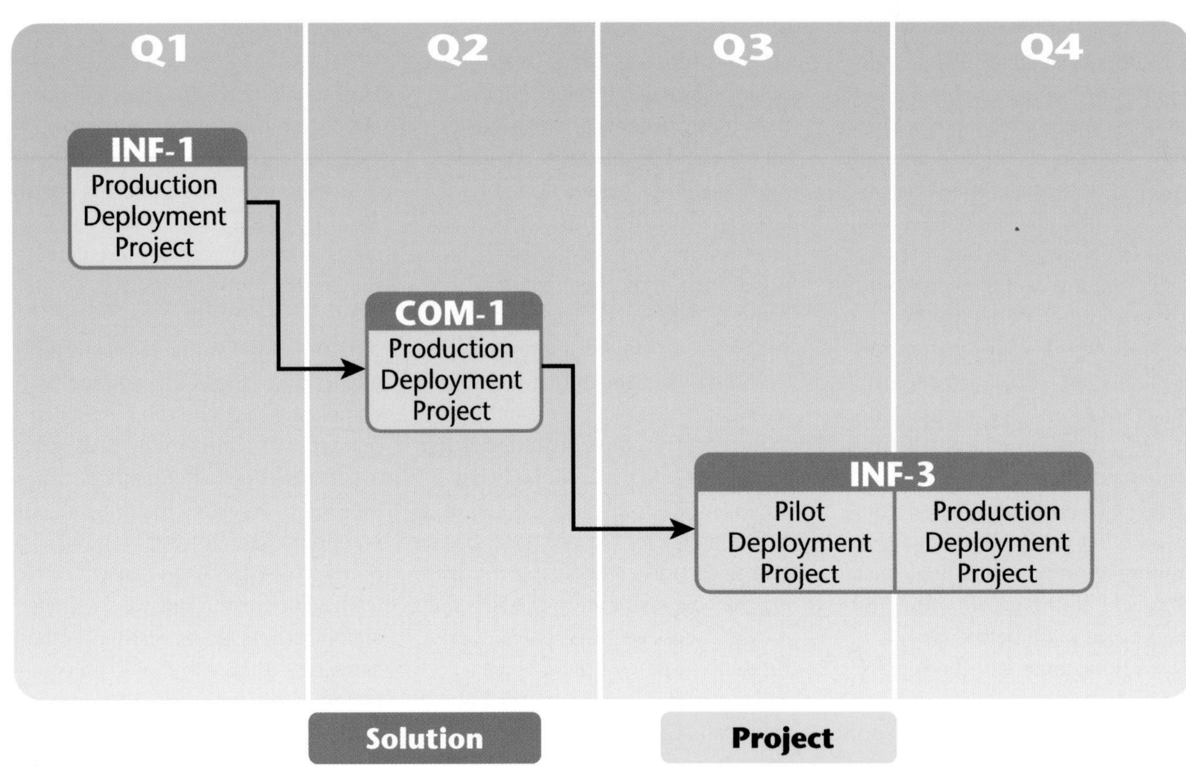

eral tools exist that help you keep track of timing, resources, and costs all in a single package. A Program Plan typically provides a high-level summary of the timing for all of the projects in a given program. **Figure 39** provides an example of how the Superior Services stakeholder program timing might be portrayed.

IT solution deployment projects often have many moving pieces that need to be kept synchronized if you are to minimize the risk of taking too much time, too much money or providing poor quality deliverables. A good project plan will help you keep all of the moving pieces together. In most cases, solution vendors will be responsible for defining and managing the project plan. In keeping with the theme of breaking down a large amount of work into bite size chunks, a good project plan features multiple phases. Phases provide synchronization points for project team deliverables and serve as good checkpoints for management needing to ensure that the project will provide the value promised in the business case. Each of our deployment project types features a slightly different set of phases **(See Figure 40).** Some of these phases can be skipped if the deliverables pertaining to the phase have already been addressed in another project, as is the case for many higher risk solution deployment projects.
A rough estimate of the effort (*See* **Table 22**) required for each of these phases can be found in the Labor section of each solution profile in **Appendix 1** under deployment costs. If you know how many resources will be available to support each phase, you will be able to estimate the overall duration of the project.

Checkpoints

If solution vendors are responsible for the project plan, make sure that you have pre-defined status checkpoints or "phase gates" for you to confirm that the project is proceeding in a manner that supports your business objectives. If you wait until the end of the project to provide an evaluation, it may be too late to make course corrections or cancel the project outright without significant timing or financial impacts.

Figure 40 Project Planning

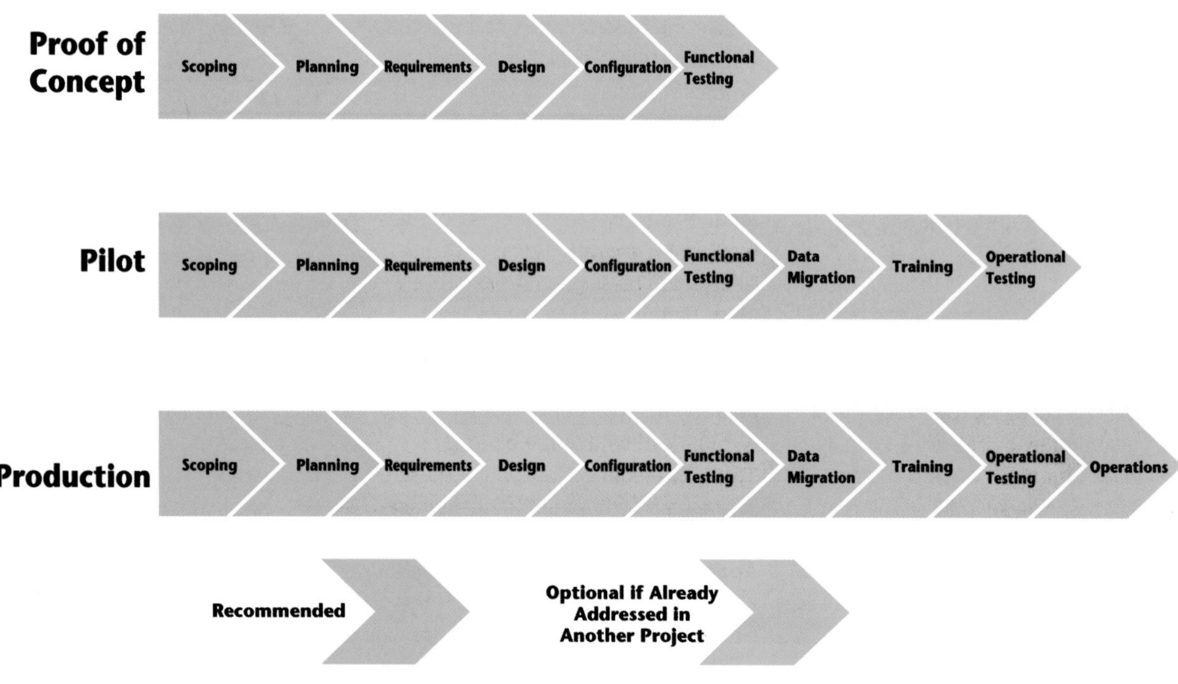

COSTS

Net Present Value

The time value of money can be reflected in business cases, but it adds a little complexity without much more value in support of the decision to proceed for most small businesses in a low inflation environment. Keep it simple – unless you are an accounting firm and you enjoy cranking a few extra numbers.

Our solution profiles also provide us with another very important set of information – costs. Cost information is presented as deployment costs and operational costs. The deployment costs translate into the rough cost of each project while the operational costs translate into the technology expenses levied on tasks within our process models. Deployment costs feature the cost of software licenses and cost of the services required to deploy the software. Services are rated according to effort. **Table 22** provides a rough estimate of the number of hours associated with each Effort Rating found in the solution profiles. The resources providing these services can be either internal resources or external resources.

If they are internal resources, you can use your internal labor costs to calculate the cost of services. If they are external resources, **Table 23** can be used to estimate the rough costs.

The operational costs reflect the costs that are incurred after the solution has been deployed. They provide a high-level summary of the projected impacts to the IT function in your organization.

Table 22 / Effort Estimates

Rating	Effort Estimate
High	>24 person-hours
Medium	8 person-hours< Effort <24 person-hours
Low	<8 person-hours

Table 23 / External Service Provider Profiles

Resource	Hourly Rates	Effort by Deployment Activity					
		Installation	Configuration	Customization	Data Migration	Training	Support
Lead Solution Consultant	$150-$350	Low	High	Low	Low	Low	Low
Lead Technical Consultant	$120-$250	High	Low	Low	Low	Low	Low
Solution Consultant	$70-$175	Low	High	Low	Low	Low	Low
Technical Consultant	$70-$150	High	Low	Low	Low	Low	Low
Trainer	$100-$150	NA	NA	NA	NA	High	NA
Technical Administrator	$75-$150	NA	NA	NA	Low	NA	High
Call Center Specialist	$50-$75	NA	NA	NA	NA	NA	High
Programmer	$75-$150	NA	NA	High	Low	NA	NA
Database Administrator	$75-$150	Low	Low	Low	High	Low	NA
Program Manager	$150-$350	Low	Low	Low	Low	Low	NA
Project Manager	$120-$250	Low	Low	Low	Low	Low	NA

With our timing plans and costs in-hand, we now have sufficient information for the evaluation of the business case for our program. A business case helps to ensure that a program makes financial sense to pursue by creating a time-based ledger of process improvement benefits against deployment and operational expenses. A sample business case is depicted in **Table 24.** If the benefits do not outweigh the expenses at some reasonable time horizon, you will save your business significant expense by stopping the pursuit of the solutions in the program. You can come back to your business case at a later time should the assumptions that drive the business case change.

Table 24 / Business Case

		Totals		Q1	Q2	Q3	Q4
Business Balance Sheet	IT Project Budget Allocation	$ 15,000		$ 5,000	$ 5,000	$ 5,000	
	Deployment Costs	$ 12,358		$ 2,160	$ 8,429	$ 1,769	$ -
	Incremental Operational Costs	$ 2,194		$ 149	$ 682	$ 682	$ 682
	Incremental Operational Benefits	$ 36,450		$ -	$ 150	$ 14,550	$ 21,750
	ROI	195%					
Solutions	**Costs**	**Operational Costs**	**Start Timing**				
INF-1	Deployment Cost	$ 2,160	Q1	$ 2,160			
	Operational Cost	$ 596	Q1	$ 149	$ 149	$ 149	$ 149
	Operational Benefits	$ 450	Q1		$ 150	$ 150	$ 150
COM-1	Deployment Cost	$ 6,550	Q2		$ 6,550		
	Operational Cost	$ 974	Q2		$ 325	$ 325	$ 325
	Operational Benefits	$ 14,400	Q2			$ 7,200	$ 7,200
INF-3	Deployment Cost	$ 3,648	Q3		$ 1,879	$ 1,769	
	Operational Cost	$ 625	Q3		$ 208	$ 208	$ 208
	Operational Benefits	$ 21,600	Q3			$ 7,200	$ 14,400

Tracking Your Journey

Since we have taken the effort to define our starting point and destination for our IT Roadmap, it makes sense that we should also track our progress as we move along towards our destination. In this spirit, you should consider conducting regular reviews of your IT Roadmap status. The minimum suggested review period varies by the scope of what you are reviewing as outlined in **Table 25.**

As your IT capabilities evolve to include business performance management tools, it will become easier to generate quality information about the status of your business on much shorter intervals. In our Superior Services example, Mike requires weekly status reports from each of his direct reports. How would you manage your business if your business metrics could be followed like a stock ticker?

Table 25 / Status Reviews

Status Review	Minimum Review Period	Sample Agenda
Business	Quarterly	Review Business Scorecard
Program	Monthly	Review Program Schedule
		Review Program Budget
		Review Program Business Case
		Review Program Issues
Process	Monthly	Review Process Scorecard
		Review Status of Programs that Impact Process
Project	Weekly	Review Project Schedule
		Review Project Budget
		Review Project Issues

When you first start to track the execution status of your IT Roadmap, the performance metrics may be no more sophisticated than smoke signals. Don't let that deter you from tracking. Your IT Roadmap can be tracked effectively in a low-tech physical War Room or high-tech virtual War Room accessible from anywhere in the world. **Figure 41** depicts an example of how the key ingredients of your IT Roadmap might be portrayed – be it on a wall or on a display screen. An IT Roadmap provides you with a wealth of information in support of management decision making. Ian converted one of the walls in his office into a "war room". The wall contains the following information:

- Current and desired performance of each functional department
- Process model diagrams for each functional department

- Summaries of all of the projects designed to change the processes complete with connections to the processes which are changed upon completion of each project

Ever since he dedicated his wall to the IT Roadmap, Ian has noticed that Mike seems to drop by more often than before. In the past, Mike's visits tended to coincide with problems that Mike was having with IT (e.g. email server crashed, laptop frozen). Now, Mike's visits were much more enjoyable. The two of them were able to spend time investigating ways to guide the business rather than react to the business. Mike made the review of the IT Roadmap a standard agenda item at his management review meetings. Soon, all of the managers began making regular visits to Ian's office to review the IT Roadmap. There was a renewed focus on the part of managers for everyone to work as a team. This new team spirit was not the rah-rah spirit found in a cheer. It was much more subtle. It was reflected in the way that each department not only completed their assigned work, they completed it in a way that met the needs of the person receiving it. The Superior Services engine was becoming tuned for high performance. Even more, the future deployments of IT solutions promised to take that performance to previously unreachable levels.

Physical to Virtual

The path for converting your physical war room to a virtual war room should start with a Business Process Management solution such as that provided by AgilePoint. Once this system is up and running, you will have access to the data that can be used to monitor Key Performance Indicators in a Business Performance Management solution such as Microsoft's Business Scorecard Manager. Enterprise Project Management solutions featuring Microsoft's Project Server software provide you with the ability to track the metrics around the agents of change for your organization – programs and projects. This suite of solutions provides you with the full scope of data found in the business information model proposed in **Step 2.**

Figure 41 Sample IT Roadmap

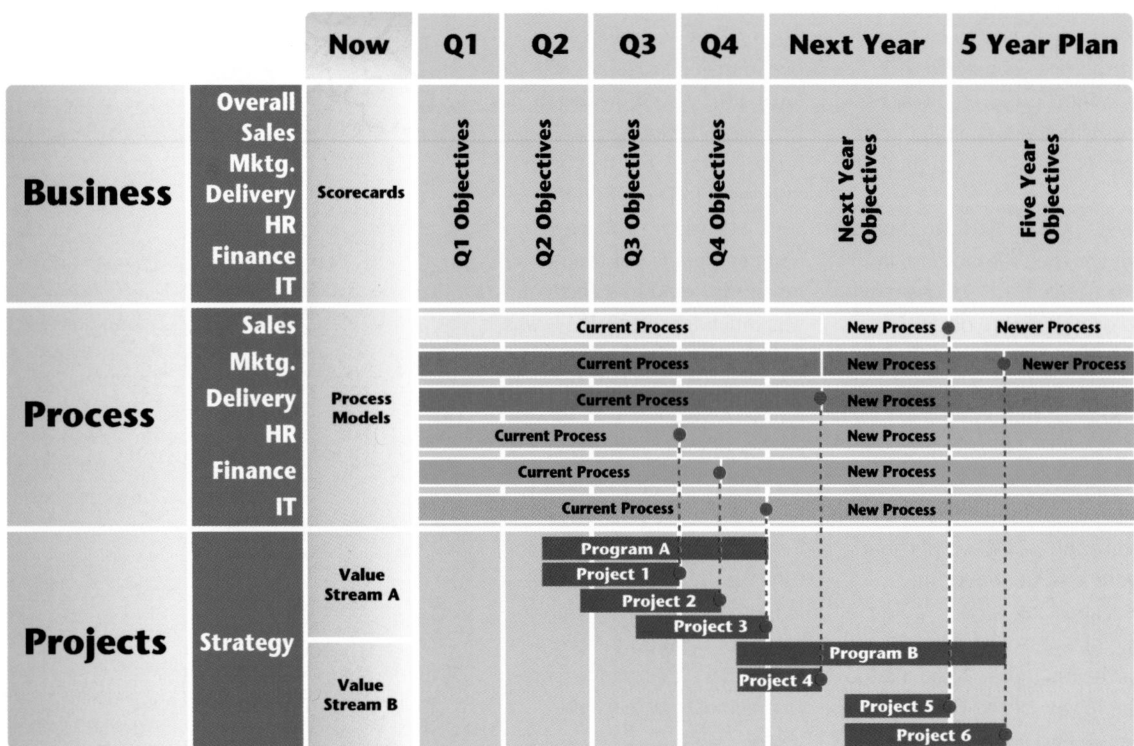

Once you have gone through the effort of defining your starting point, don't forget the importance of that friendly "You are Here" sign. Ensure via your periodic reviews that your projects still support your process improvement objectives. Don't be afraid to kill a project that is not going according to plan. Good project management practices should provide you with ample warning to avoid surprises.

Travel Advisories

Another way to avoid surprises is to expect them. There are risks associated with venturing into the world of IT with your roadmap. Awareness of these risks before taking off on your journey will help to ensure that you avoid the more serious pitfalls on your journey. **Table 26** provides a summary of some of the situations that could send you off course as well as advice that should help keep you on track.

"Obstacles are those frightful things you see when you take your eyes off your goal"
- Henry Ford

Table 26 / Travel Advisories

Risk	Description	Advice
Problem Creators	Some solution providers can actually be problem creators. Be wary of service providers that talk technology before talking about your business. They may be well intentioned, but unless they provide a solution that meets your business needs, you will have simply purchased an expensive paperweight with flashing lights.	The key to avoiding a poor supplier is to first be a good customer. The clear definition of your expectations using the tools outlined in this book is invaluable. Be wary of solution providers who seek to deploy the technology without an attempt to understand these expectations. Look for Microsoft Certified Partners at Microsoft.com.
Business Disruption	You may think that by having a third party solution provider deploy a solution, you can avoid any disruptions to your business operations. If so, you are mistaken. During solution deployment, solution providers will require the support of many of the key personnel in your organization for requirements definition, testing, and validation that the solution will work in your organization as intended. In addition, many solutions require the migration of data that could result in a more serious disruption of business operations.	Ensure that the solution provider starts the project with a detailed plan that defines who from your organization is needed and when. Confirm that your employees will be able to support the dates specified or adjust the dates accordingly. Once you confirm your support dates, ensure that you honor them. Every cancelled appointment is likely to stretch out the deployment timing and, remember, time is money.

Table 26 / Travel Advisories (Continued)

Risk	Description	Advice
Technology Interoperability	There are many competing technology platforms and technology vendors available. If you attempt to insert a square solution peg into your round infrastructure hole be prepared for some nasty surprises. Many of these surprises result in a reduction in the number of solution features that can be used or even create issues with existing software or capabilities (e.g. remote access).	Stick with a single technology platform. Microsoft offers a variety of "People Ready" products tailored to meet the needs of small businesses. Microsoft has a strong partner community that can not only help ensure the effective deployment of Microsoft solutions, but also provide a host of their own solutions that have been designed to work well with Microsoft software.
Security	Your Information Technology manages a lot of information – much of it highly sensitive or critical to your business operations. What would be the impact to your business if an unauthorized party had access to your data? What if you were to lose some of your data?	Ensure that you always apply the latest security patches to your solutions.
		Ensure that you have an effective data backup plan in operation.
		Ensure that you have a disaster recovery plan.
Scalability	You are a small business today, but you may like to be a big business tomorrow. Will your solutions scale with you, or will you have to hit the reset button?	Ask your solution provider for a list of conditions that would lead to unsatisfactory performance levels. If these levels are unknown, you may wish to pursue performance testing as an element of the solution provider statement of work.
Custom Solutions	Basic configuration of off–shelf solutions will not satisfy the needs of your business so you decide to pursue a custom solution. Custom solutions are notoriously tricky to implement – especially for organizations that are new or averse to clearly defined requirements specifications.	Use your process models and value streams as the basis of your requirements specifications for solution providers.
		Ensure that you have access to the source code if the company should go out of business or fail to honor any warranty that you may have negotiated. Software escrow accounts can be setup to achieve this goal.
IT for the Sake of IT	Being technology savvy is a risk itself. Technology's shiny objects can appear quite compelling. If you don't have a tangible understanding of how a solution will impact your overall business operations before deploying it, you may adversely impact the performance of your business.	Follow the steps outlined in the IT Roadmap.

Step 5 Review

A wide range of considerations go into deploying IT solutions. It is not simple to get from where you are to where you need to be.
If you are overwhelmed, remember that professionals can help if they know what you want to achieve. Even if you don't have all of the answers, it is often quite useful to understand all of the key questions.

Start with asking yourself
...What kind of solutions do I need to meet my performance objectives?
...What kind of IT organization do I want my business to have?
...What is the value of implementing these solutions?
...What are the keys ingredients to deploying these solutions with a minimum of risk?

The guidelines provided in this section should help you engage solution vendors with confidence.

You have now passed by the following IT Roadmap milestones:

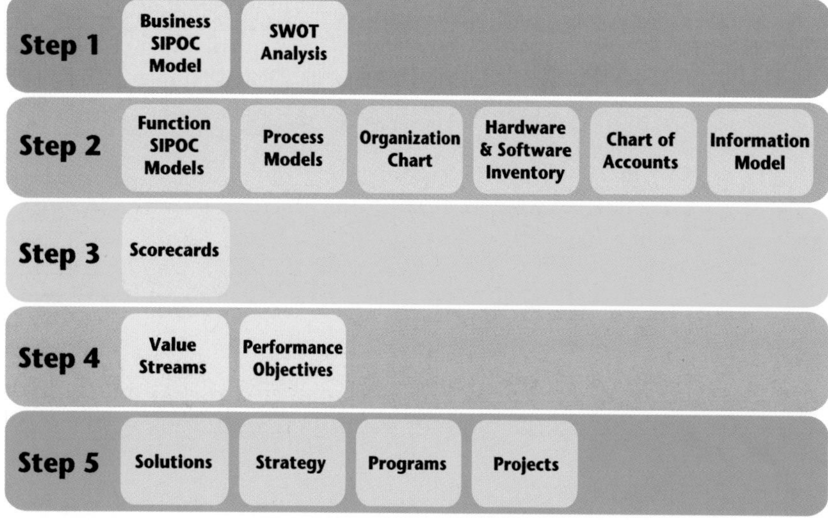

IT ROADMAP IN REVIEW

"This great increase of the quantity of work, which, in consequence of the division of labour, the same number of people are capable of performing, is owing to three different circumstances; first, to the increase of dexterity in every particular workman; secondly, to the saving of the time which is commonly lost in passing from one species of work to another; and lastly, to the invention of a great number of machines which facilitate and abridge labour, and enable one man to do the work of many".

Adam Smith, *The Wealth of Nations.* (Circa 1776)

It may be hard to believe, but Adam Smith set the stage for the Information Technology Roadmap over 230 years ago.

- Increase the skills of your workforce.
- Avoid losing time in transitions between types of work.
- Implement technology where it makes sense to "enable one man to do the work of many".

Do these statements ring true for your business today?

The key to improving your business is not technology in and of itself. Computers and software are simply some of the most recent tools for improving our productivity or, as Adam Smith calls it, "quantity of work". The key to improving the performance of your business is to understand what you do and then seek to make systematic improvements to what you do. The IT Roadmap provides this key.

In **Step 1,** we provided an outsider's view of a Professional Services Firm business model.

In **Step 2,** we provided an insider's view of a Professional Services Firm business model.

In **Step 3,** we learned how to apply financial measurements to our business model.

In **Step 4,** we learned how to identify pragmatic opportunities to improve the performance of our business.

In **Step 5,** we covered how to take advantage of those opportunities and implement our IT strategy. ▶

Implementing the IT Roadmap is not much of a stretch for most businesses in concept – only in practice.
Most of the construction tools already exist in most businesses. Process flows can be found. Organization charts can be found. A Chart of Accounts can be found. What is rare to see is someone or something that shows how they all fit together.

What's even rarer is to see someone or something that can show how they all tie to the performance of the business as in **Figure 42.**

Figure 42 Connected Complexity

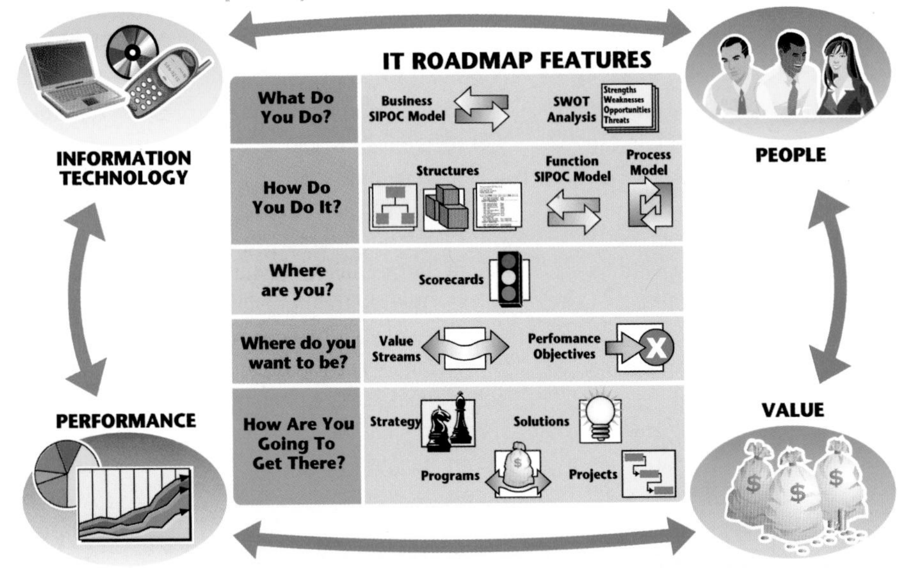

Most IT vendors are not aware of how all of these components fit together for your business. If you have yet to develop an IT Roadmap, perhaps even you don't know how they fit together. To be effective, your information technology does need to know these connections. You will pave a road filled with successful IT deployment projects if you can successfully connect the dots.

As you drive off to develop an IT Roadmap tailored to your business, keep the following road signs in mind:

- Understand what you are changing from before you change to something else.
- Small businesses can appear to be big businesses with the right technology.
- Ensure that the business drives the technology, not the other way around.
- Focus the information you gather on the decisions you need to make
- Develop mutually rewarding relationships with one or more IT solution providers.

If you implement the roadmap outlined within this book you are on your way to happier customers, happier employees
and happier stakeholders.

Happy trails!

APPENDIX 1: SOLUTION PROFILES

This appendix includes profiles for a sample of software-based solutions. These profiles can be used to jump-start the development of your IT strategy using the steps outlined as part of the IT Roadmap. Once you have identified the gap between your current performance and desired performance in context of your value streams, **Table 19** can be used to develop a short list of solutions that might be suitable to fill the gap. Review the profiles for the solutions of interest and contact the listed vendors for more information on how to implement the solution. These sample solutions have been ordered in **Appendix 1** in the same sequence applied in **Table 19.**

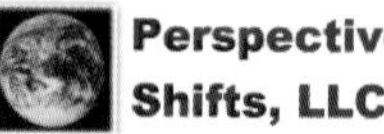

IMPORTANT NOTES ON SOLUTION PROFILES:

- **All prices shown are in US dollars unless otherwise noted. Prices are estimates only based on information available at the time of printing. Contact an authorized solution provider for pricing specific to your business needs (See Microsoft Solution Builder reference in Appendix 3).**
- **Microsoft product screen shots reprinted with permission from Microsoft Corporation.**
- **Screen shots are intended to provide an overview of the look and feel of the pertinent solution as it would appear to an end user. They are not intended to assist in comparative assessments of the solution with other solutions.**
- **Microsoft sponsorship should not be inferred by the inclusion of 3rd party solutions within the list of profiles.**
- **All 3rd party solutions have been provided by registered Microsoft partners.**
- **The URL's provided in this book were active at the time of printing. Pages may have been moved since this book was printed. If a link address does not contain the information referenced, type in the root of the URL (e.g. www.microsoft.com) and navigate through the site until you find the desired information or use any search capabilities provided at the site.**

BPM-1 Business Scorecard Manager Screen Shot

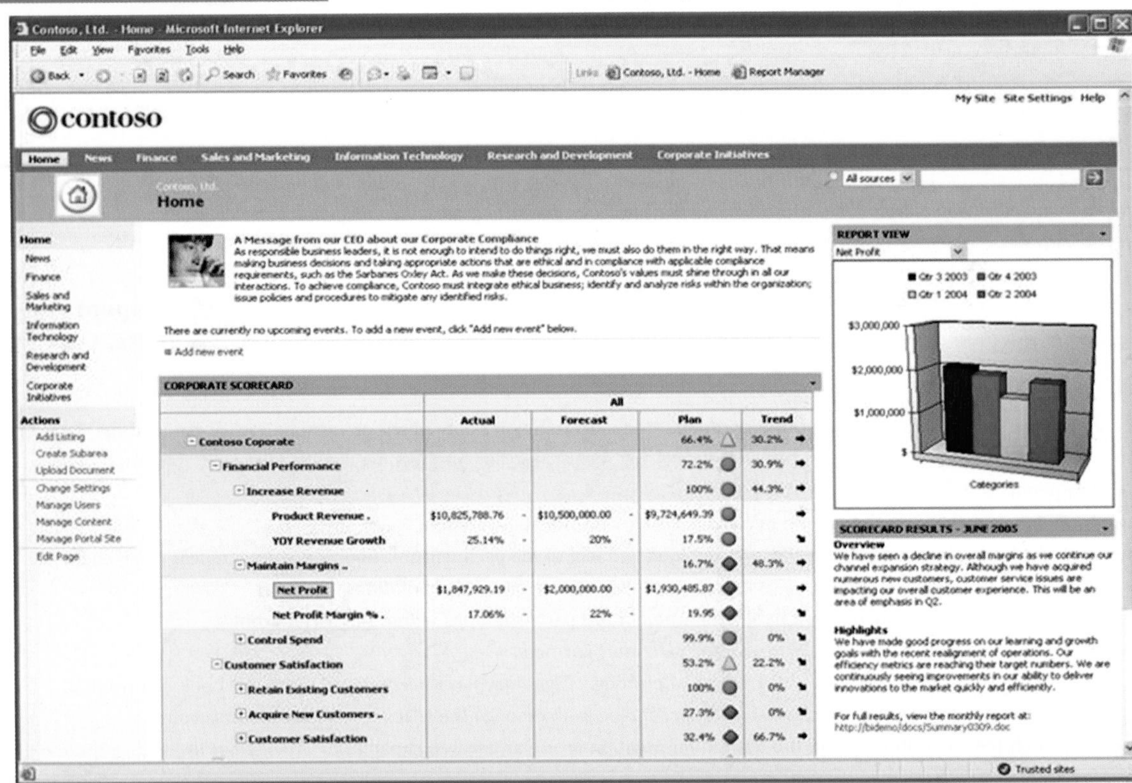

BPM-1 Business Scorecard Manager Profile

Solution ID	Solution Title	Solution Provider	Solution Category
BPM-1	Business Scorecard Manager	Microsoft (www.microsoft.com)	Business Performance Management

Solution Description

Business Scorecard Manager provides you with the ability to display Key Performance Indicator metrics from multiple data sources within a consolidated scorecard. Users are able to drill down into the data behind the metrics in an easy-to-use manner using the Internet Explorer web browser.

Software

Title	Vendor	Product Info	Dependencies
Business Scorecard Manager	Microsoft	http://office.microsoft.com/en-us/FX012225041033.aspx	INF-1, COM-1, INF-2, INF-4

Costs

Deployment Costs				Operating Costs			
Labor Expenses		Technology Expenses		Labor Expenses		Technology Expenses	
		Software Licensing					
Task	Effort	Cost	Type	Task	Effort		
Installation	Medium	$175 $4,999 (SOURCE: Microsoft.com)	User or Device Server	**Configuration Administration**	Medium	**Upgrades**	Contact Microsoft partners about Software Assurance program benefits and eligibility.
Configuration	Medium			**Technical Administration**	Medium	**Incremental Users**	External connector license enables an unlimited number of non-employees to access the server for $30,000.
Customization	NA						
Data Migration	Low						
Training	Low						

More Information

You can find Microsoft Partners near you to help you deploy solutions for your business at https://www.microsoft.com/smallbusiness/products/solution-advisor.mspx.
Additional Business Performance Management solutions are planned by Microsoft for 2007 including enhanced Analytics and Planning functionality.
For more information search for PerformancePoint Server at Microsoft.com.

PRO-1 AgilePoint Screen Shot

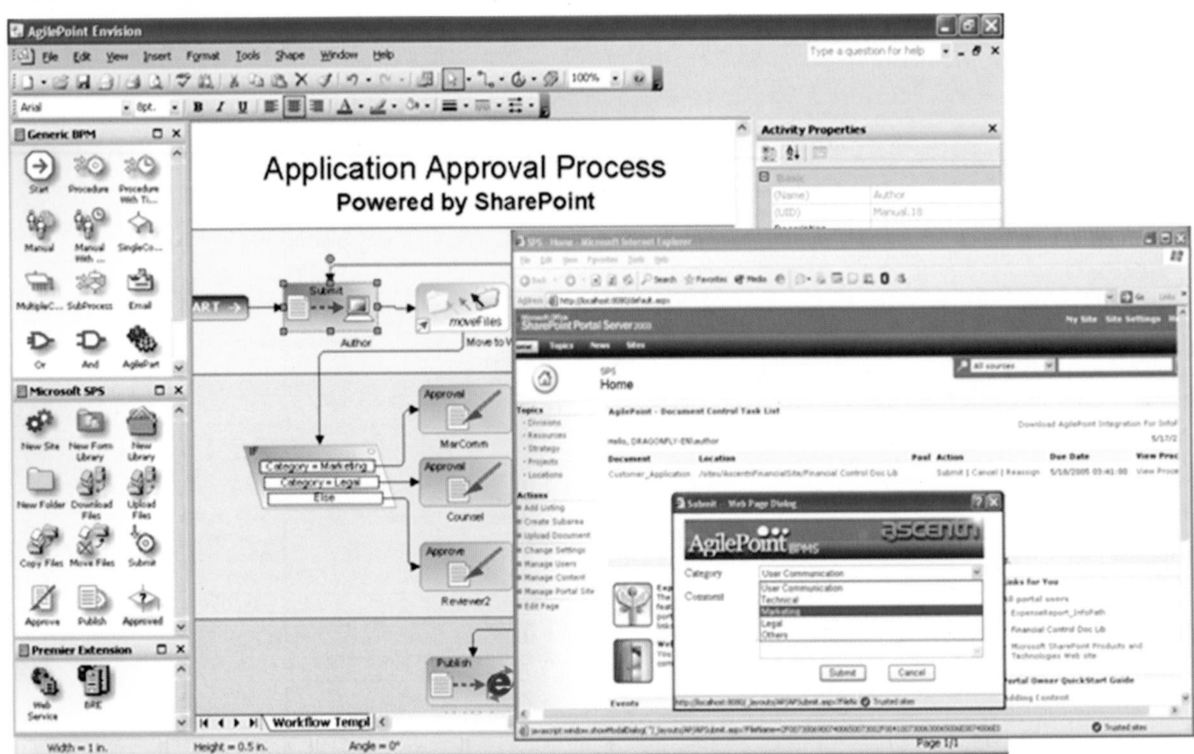

PRO-1 AgilePoint Profile

Solution ID	Solution Title	Solution Provider	Solution Category
PRO-1	AgilePoint BPMS	Ascentn (www.ascentn.com)	Business Process Management

Solution Description

AgilePoint BPMS software suite enables any business to automate workflows and end-to-end business processes by simply diagramming a process model using a popular diagramming tool such as Microsoft Visio. This means any business can quickly realize the benefits of business process automation without a large IT staff and deep pockets.

AgilePoint provides significant value to businesses by allowing them to:

1. Reuse their existing Microsoft investments and skill sets, which saves time, money and reduces risk.
2. Convert their business operations into technical assets with minimum technical knowledge and reuse them in the form of easy -to-understand process icons representing reusable business activities.
3. Create a library of reusable business processes that can be quickly assembled by non-technical users to deliver business automation needs.

AgilePoint delivers the industry's most cost-effective business process management solution, extending affordability to small-and mid-sized organizations.

Software

Title	Vendor	Product Info	Dependencies
AgilePoint Envision	Ascentn	http://www.ascentn.com/Products/envision.html	INF-1, Microsoft Visio
AgilePoint Developer (OPTIONAL)	Ascentn	http://www.ascentn.com/Products/developer.html	INF-1, INF-2, Visual Studio
AgilePoint Server	Ascentn	http://www.ascentn.com/Products/server.html	INF-2
AgilePoint Enterprise Manager	Ascentn	http://www.ascentn.com/Products/enterprise.html	INF-1, INF-2

Costs

Deployment Costs

Labor Expenses		Technology Expenses	
		Software Licensing	
Task	Effort	Cost	Type
Installation	Low	$8,590 for Starter Edition	Non-Standard: 5 Business Processes (unlimited instances) and Up To 20 Concurrent Users
Configuration	Medium	$18,950 for Professional Edition	Non-Standard: 50 Business Processes (unlimited instances) and Up To 100 Concurrent Users
Customization	NA		
Data Migration	Medium		
Training	Medium		

Operating Costs

Labor Expenses		Technology Expenses	
Task	Effort		
Configuration Administration	Medium	**Upgrades**	Contact Ascentn directly or AgilePoint Service Provider (see below).
Technical Administration	Low	**Incremental Users**	Contact Ascentn directly or AgilePoint Service Provider (see below).

More Information

There are multiple configurations of AgilePoint available to meet your specific needs, including an On-Demand Hosting Service that makes it easier for small businesses to get started. The following AgilePoint Service Providers can help you identify and deploy the solution configuration that works best for your business: B2BTechnologies (www.b2btech.com), Intellinet (www.intellinet.com), Intrasight (www.intrasight.net), KSMLogics (www.ksmlogics.com), DigiPoint (www.digipoint.be), ARES Int'l (www.ares.com.tw), DirectPointe (www.directpointe.com), OptimusBP (www.optimusBT.com). Service Providers should be contacted if you would like to use the optional AgilePoint Developer component as it requires programming skills.

PRO-2 BizTalk Screen Shot

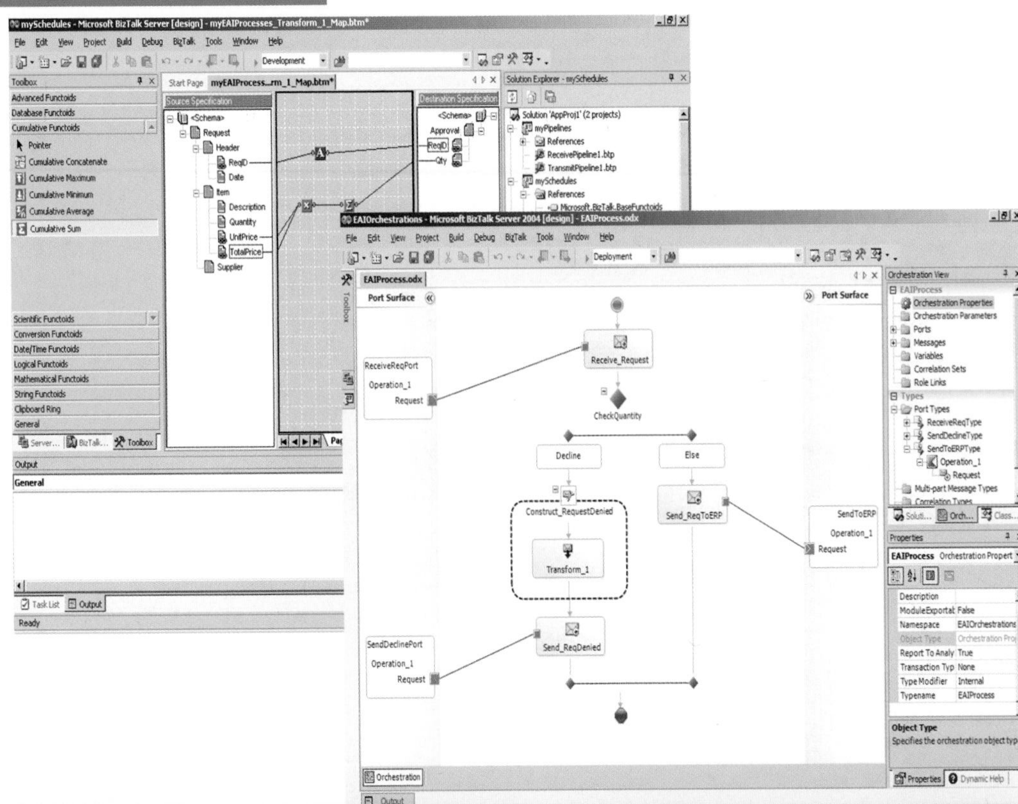

PRO-2 BizTalk Profile

Solution ID	Solution Title	Solution Provider	Solution Category
PRO-2	BizTalk	Microsoft (www.microsoft.com)	Business Process Management

Solution Description

BizTalk helps you efficiently and effectively integrate systems, employees, and trading partners through manageable business processes, letting you automate and orchestrate interactions in a highly flexible and automated manner (SOURCE: microsoft.com).

Software

Title	Vendor	Product Info	Dependencies
BizTalk Server	Microsoft	http://www.microsoft.com/biztalk/default.mspx	INF-2, COM-1, INF-4, Visual Studio

Costs

Deployment Costs				Operating Costs			
Labor Expenses		Technology Expenses		Labor Expenses		Technology Expenses	
		Software Licensing					
Task	Effort	Cost	Type	Task	Effort		
Installation	Medium	$8,499 for Standard Edition $29,999 for Enterprise Edition (SOURCE: microsoft.com)	Per processor Per processor	**Configuration Administration**	High	**Upgrades**	Contact Microsoft partners about Software Assurance program benefits and eligibility.
Configuration	High			**Technical Administration**	Medium	**Incremental Users**	Contact Microsoft partners about Volume Licensing program.
Customization	High						
Data Migration	Medium						

More Information

You can find Microsoft Partners near you to help you deploy solutions for your business at https://www.microsoft.com/smallbusiness/products/solution-advisor.mspx. Microsoft ISV (Independent Solution Vendor) partners offer many products that supplement the core BizTalk functionality.
More information can be found at microsoft.com.

COM-1 Microsoft Office Screen Shot

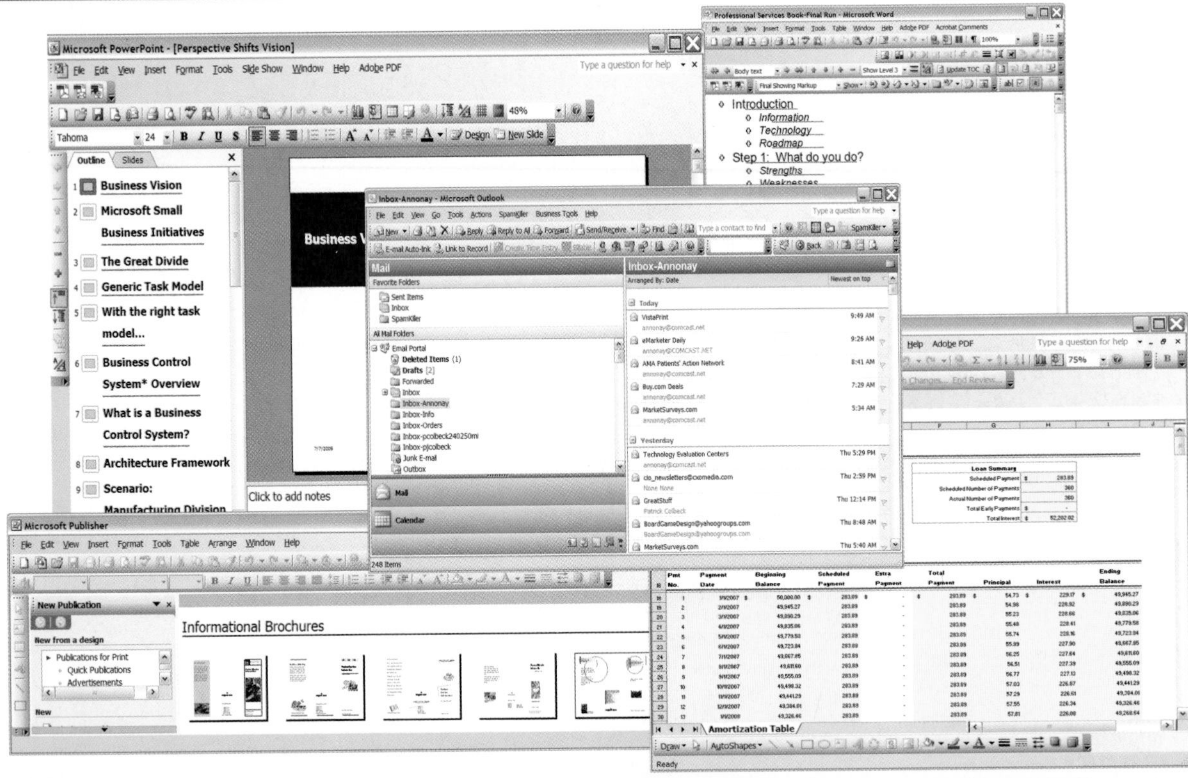

COM-1 Microsoft Office Profile

Solution ID	Solution Title	Solution Provider	Solution Category
COM-1	Microsoft Office Small Business Edition	Microsoft (www.microsoft.com)	Collaboration

Solution Description

The Microsoft Office Small Business Edition features the applications that most small businesses need the most. The tool suite includes information that will help manage finances and customer relationships along with the core collaboration features inherent in the Microsoft Office System.

Software

Title	Vendor	Product Info	Dependencies
Excel	Microsoft	http://www.microsoft.com/office/excel/prodinfo/default.mspx	INF-1
Outlook	Microsoft	http://www.microsoft.com/office/outlook/prodinfo/default.mspx	INF-1
Outlook with Business Contact Manager Update	Microsoft	http://www.microsoft.com/office/outlook/contactmanager/prodinfo/default.mspx	INF-1
PowerPoint	Microsoft	http://www.microsoft.com/office/powerpoint/prodinfo/default.mspx	INF-1
Publisher	Microsoft	http://www.microsoft.com/office/publisher/prodinfo/default.mspx	INF-1
Word	Microsoft	http://www.microsoft.com/office/word/prodinfo/default.mspx	INF-1

Costs

Deployment Costs

Labor Expenses: Task	Effort	Technology Expenses – Software Licensing: Cost	Type
Installation	Low	$639 (SOURCE: Microsoft.com)	User
Configuration	Low		
Customization	NA		
Data Migration	Low		
Training	Low		

Operating Costs

Labor Expenses: Task	Effort	Technology Expenses	
Configuration Administration	Low	**Upgrades**	$469 per user or investigate Microsoft Software Assurance program.
Technical Administration	Low	**Incremental Users**	See Microsoft Authorized Resellers for volume discount pricing and incentives.

More Information

The Microsoft Office System is available in many different editions. Please see http://www.microsoft.com/office/editions/howtobuy/compare.mspx for more information on which solution might best fit your business needs.

Microsoft offers a significant number of free downloads that help maximize the value of your software purchase. You are encouraged to investigate the templates, clip art and media, and downloads section of the Microsoft Office System homepage at Microsoft.com (http://office.microsoft.com/en-us/default.aspx).

COM-2 Live Meeting Screen Shot

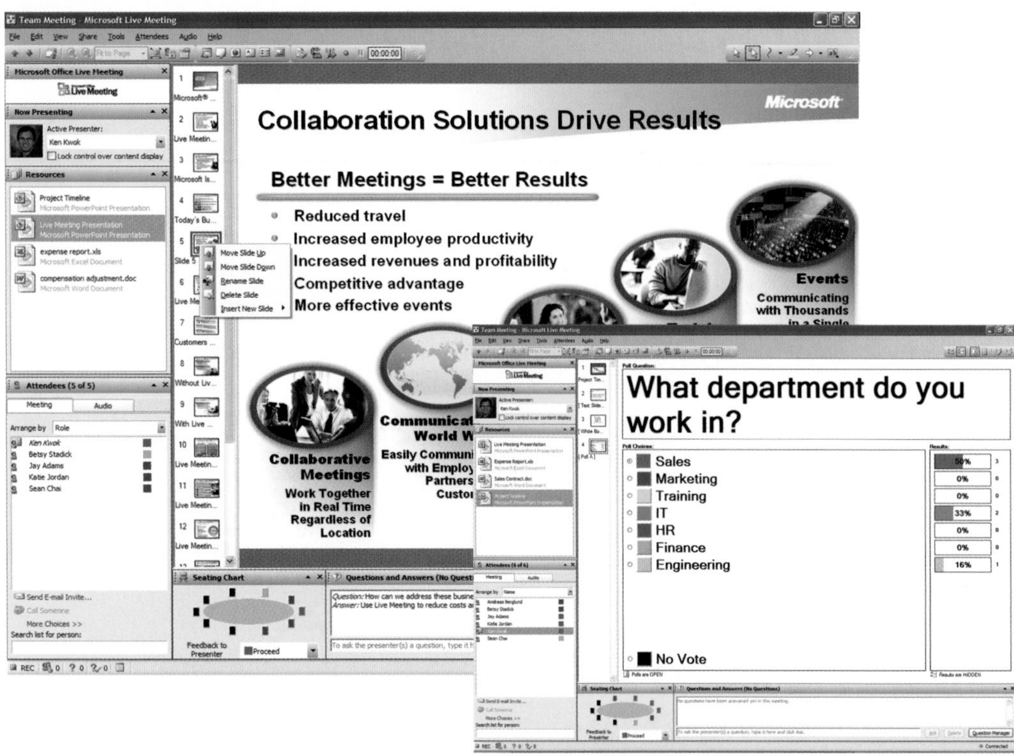

COM-2 Live Meeting Profile

<table>
<tr><th>Solution ID</th><th colspan="3">Solution Title</th><th colspan="2">Solution Provider</th><th colspan="2">Solution Category</th></tr>
<tr><td>COM-2</td><td colspan="3">Live Meeting</td><td colspan="2">Microsoft (www.microsoft.com)</td><td colspan="2">Collaboration</td></tr>
<tr><th colspan="8">Solution Description</th></tr>
<tr><td colspan="8">Live Meeting is a hosted web conferencing service offered by Microsoft. Live Meeting has no server software to install or deploy. Anyone can participate in a Live Meeting using just a PC, an internet connection, and a telephone. Meeting sessions can be recorded for on-demand play back, making it an ideal medium for conducting training courses.</td></tr>
<tr><th colspan="8">Software</th></tr>
<tr><th>Title</th><th>Vendor</th><th colspan="4">Product Info</th><th colspan="2">Dependencies</th></tr>
<tr><td>Live Meeting</td><td>Microsoft</td><td colspan="4">http://office.microsoft.com/en-us/FX010909711033.aspx</td><td colspan="2">INF-1 and COM-1 are recommended</td></tr>
<tr><th colspan="8">Costs</th></tr>
<tr><th colspan="4">Deployment Costs</th><th colspan="4">Operating Costs</th></tr>
<tr><th colspan="2">Labor Expenses</th><th colspan="2">Technology Expenses</th><th colspan="2">Labor Expenses</th><th colspan="2" rowspan="3">Technology Expenses</th></tr>
<tr><th rowspan="2">Task</th><th rowspan="2">Effort</th><th colspan="2">Software Licensing</th><th rowspan="2">Task</th><th rowspan="2">Effort</th></tr>
<tr><th>Cost</th><th>Type</th></tr>
<tr><td>Installation</td><td>NA</td><td rowspan="5">$180 for Standard Edition
$300 for Professional Edition
$3,000</td><td rowspan="5">User
User
Service</td><td>Configuration Administration</td><td>NA</td><td>Upgrades</td><td>Not applicable</td></tr>
<tr><td>Configuration</td><td>NA</td><td rowspan="4">Technical Administration</td><td rowspan="4">NA</td><td rowspan="4">Incremental Users</td><td rowspan="4">$375/month for 5 users
$750/month for 10 users
$0.35/minute with unlimited users</td></tr>
<tr><td>Customization</td><td>NA</td></tr>
<tr><td>Data Migration</td><td>NA</td></tr>
<tr><td>Training</td><td>Low</td></tr>
<tr><th colspan="8">More Information</th></tr>
<tr><td colspan="8">Live Meeting is an early example of an initiative at Microsoft to provide Software as a Service. Go to the LiveMeeting section of Microsoft.com to sign up.</td></tr>
</table>

CRM-1 Results Business Suite Screen Shot

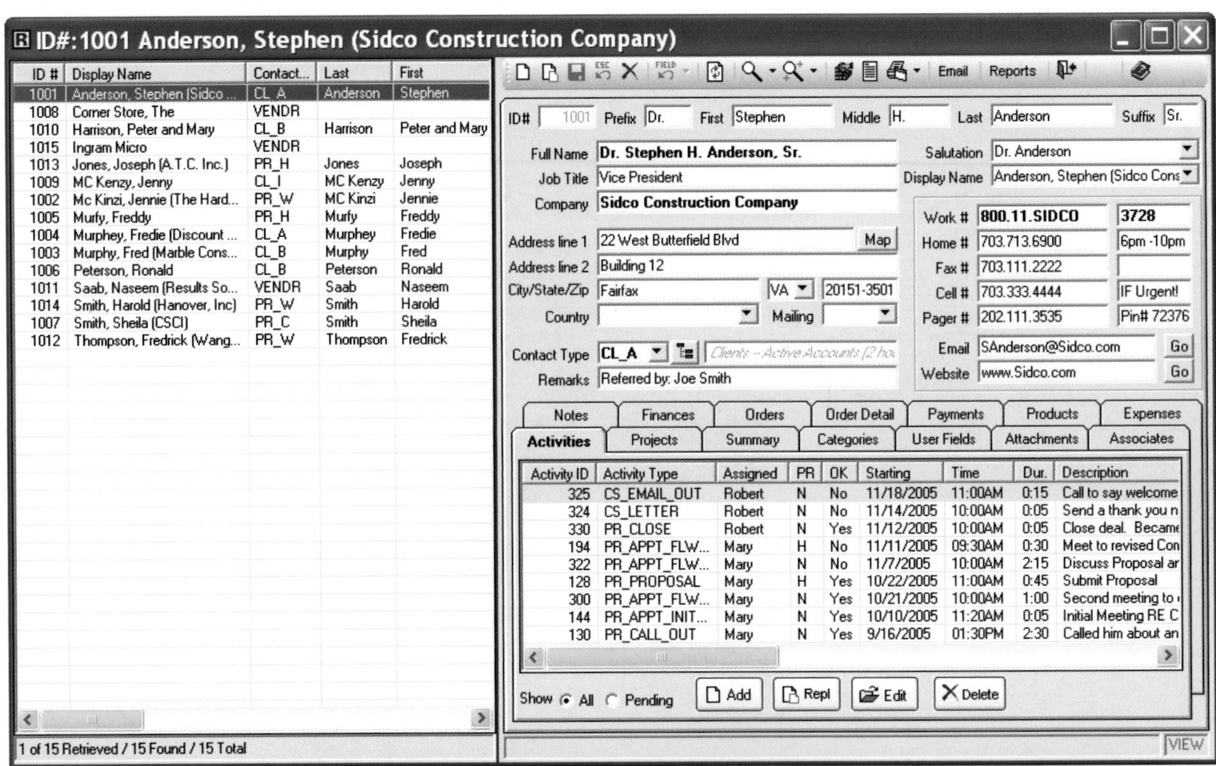

CRM-1 Results Business Suite Profile

Solution ID	Solution Title	Solution Provider	Solution Category
CRM-1	Results Business Suite	Results Software (www.Results-Software.com)	Customer Relationship Management

Solution Description

Results Business Suite helps you manage and grow your business by combining Customer Relationship Management (CRM) and business management in one integrated solution. Results Business Suite includes the front-office functionality of our popular Results CRM solution with back-office features that includes integrated time billing, invoicing, payments, inventory and expense tracking. This solution dramatically improves efficiency and communication across all departments within your organization. With this cohesive 360 degree view of customer and prospect relationships and of your business, you receive instant access to all relevant data. Results Business Suite provides all this in one comprehensive solution, whether you're working in the office or remotely via the web.

The Results Business Suite: improves customer relationships and value; enhances your professional image; integrates with QuickBooks®; boosts revenue by integrating time-billing and invoicing; manages your customer and prospect information; provides a wealth of reporting tools; enhances communication and productivity; delivers an affordable software solution; expedites payment collection; allows your sales department to upsell; improves customer service; helps your small business grow; scalable solution to accommodate your current budget and planned growth; one solution for the mobile and traditional workforce.

Software

Title	Vendor	Product Info	Dependencies
Results Business Suite	Results Software	http://www.results-software.com/Products/Business_Suite/	INF-1. Note: Will also work with older versions of Windows® like 95, 98, ME and 2000.

Costs

Deployment Costs

Labor Expenses		Technology Expenses	
Task	Effort	Software Licensing	
		Cost	Type
Installation	Low	From $895 to $1,295	Named-User or Concurrent Option
Configuration	Medium		
Customization	Low		
Data Migration	Medium		
Training	Low		

Operating Costs

Labor Expenses		Technology Expenses	
Task	Effort		
Configuration Administration	Low	**Upgrades**	20%
Technical Administration	Low	**Incremental Users**	Volume Discount

More Information

Results-Software also offers an On-Demand version that provides a simple entry point for small businesses.
Contact Results-Software at www.Results-Software.com for more information.

CRM-2 Microsoft Dynamics™ CRM Screen Shot

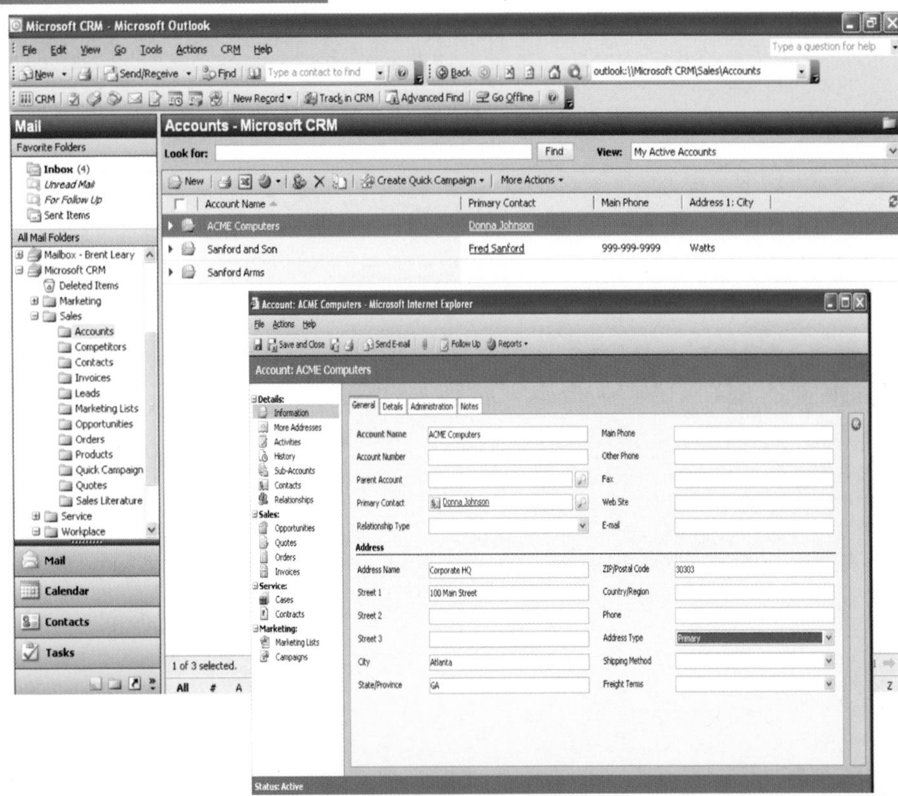

CRM-2 Microsoft Dynamics™ CRM Profile

Solution ID	Solution Title	Solution Providers	Solution Category
CRM-2	Microsoft Customer Relationship Management	CRM Essentials (www.crm-essentials.com) or The Norwich Group (www.thenorwichgroup.com)	Customer Relationship Management

Solution Description

Microsoft Dynamics™ CRM 3.0 Small Business Edition is the latest version of Microsoft's CRM software built specifically for small businesses. CRM's main purpose is to increase productivity and profitability through better, more meaningful interactions with current and prospective customers. The software features detailed "relationship" tracking including prospects, customers, vendors, suppliers, referral sources and invalidated leads. Also includes service and trouble ticket tracking, article and knowledge base library, integration to e-mail, preparation of quotes, detailed product/ resource management and scheduling. Has the unique ability to be configured to fit unique business models.

Software

Title	Vendor	Product Info	Dependencies
Dynamics™ CRM	Microsoft	http://www.microsoft.com/dynamics/crm/default.mspx	INF-1, INF-3 (Premium)

Costs

Deployment Costs				Operating Costs			
Labor Expenses		Technology Expenses		Labor Expenses		Technology Expenses	
		Software Licensing					
Task	Effort	Cost	Type	Task	Effort		
Installation	Low	$599 for Small Business Edition $499 for Small Business Edition	Server User	**Configuration Administration**	Low	**Upgrades**	Software Assurance Program included for 1 year.
Configuration	Medium			**Technical Administration**	Low	**Incremental Users**	Volume discounts and incentives are available through an Authorized Reseller.
Customization	NA						
Data Migration	Medium						
Training	Low						

More Information

Solution Providers: CRM Essentials (crm-essentials.com), The Norwich Group (thenorwichgroup.com)
Blogs: http://thenorwichgroup.blogs.com/mscrm
Books: *Working with Microsoft Dynamics™ CRM 3.0* by Mike Snyder, Jim Steger; *Microsoft CRM 3 For Dummies* by Joel Scott, David Lee; *Special Edition Using Microsoft CRM* by Laura Brown, John Gravely
User Groups: Microsoft CRM Newsgroup (http://www.microsoft.com/Businesssolutions/Community/Newsgroups/dgbrowser/en-us/default.mspx?dg=microsoft.public.crm&lang=en&cr=US); MS CRM Study Group (http://finance.groups.yahoo.com/group/MSCRMStudy/); MS CRM User Group (http://groups.yahoo.com/group/mscrm_smb/)

CRM-3 Microsoft Dynamics™ CRM Live Screen Shot

Coming Soon!

Screen Shot not available at time of printing.
Product availability scheduled for 2007.
Appearance anticipated to be similar to Dynamics CRM except it will be web-based.

CRM-3 Microsoft Dynamics™ CRM Live Profile

<table>
<tr><th>Solution ID</th><th colspan="2">Solution Title</th><th colspan="3">Solution Providers</th><th colspan="2">Solution Category</th></tr>
<tr><td>CRM-3</td><td colspan="2">Microsoft Dynamics(TM) CRM Live</td><td colspan="3">Microsoft (www.microsoft.com)</td><td colspan="2">Customer Relationship Management</td></tr>
<tr><th colspan="8">Solution Description</th></tr>
<tr><td colspan="8">Microsoft Dynamics™ CRM Live uses the same code base as the Microsoft Dynamics™ CRM product but provides its functionality via the Software as a Service delivery model. Software as a Service saves customers the need to manage their own infrastructure. The software will be hosted with Microsoft's own data centers. Users will access the functionality provided by the software via their web browser and an internet connection.

CRM's main purpose is to increase productivity and profitability through better, more meaningful interactions with current and prospective customers. The software features detailed "Relationship" tracking including Prospects, Customers, Vendors, Suppliers, Referral Sources and invalidated Leads. Also includes service and trouble ticket tracking, article and knowledge base library, integration to e-mail, preparation of quotes, detailed product, resource management and scheduling.
Has the unique ability to be configured to fit unique business models.</td></tr>
<tr><th colspan="8">Software</th></tr>
<tr><th>Title</th><th>Vendor</th><th colspan="4">Product Info</th><th colspan="2">Dependencies</th></tr>
<tr><td>Dynamics™ CRM Live</td><td>Microsoft</td><td colspan="4">http://www.crmlive.com</td><td colspan="2">INF-1</td></tr>
<tr><th colspan="8">Costs</th></tr>
<tr><th colspan="4">Deployment Costs</th><th colspan="4">Operating Costs</th></tr>
<tr><th colspan="2">Labor Expenses</th><th colspan="2">Technology Expenses</th><th colspan="2">Labor Expenses</th><th colspan="2">Technology Expenses</th></tr>
<tr><th>Task</th><th>Effort</th><th colspan="2">Software Licensing</th><th>Task</th><th>Effort</th><th colspan="2"></th></tr>
<tr><th></th><th></th><th>Cost</th><th>Type</th><th></th><th></th><th colspan="2"></th></tr>
<tr><td>Installation</td><td>NA</td><td rowspan="5">Contact a Microsoft Solution Partner for solution-based pricing</td><td rowspan="5">Contact a Microsoft Solution Partner for solution-based pricing</td><td>Configuration Administration</td><td>NA</td><td>Upgrades</td><td>NA</td></tr>
<tr><td>Configuration</td><td>Medium</td><td rowspan="4">Technical Administration</td><td rowspan="4">NA</td><td rowspan="4">Incremental Users</td><td rowspan="4">Contact a Microsoft Solution Partner for solution-based pricing</td></tr>
<tr><td>Customization</td><td>NA</td></tr>
<tr><td>Data Migration</td><td>Medium</td></tr>
<tr><td>Training</td><td>Low</td></tr>
<tr><th colspan="8">More Information</th></tr>
<tr><td colspan="8">Dynamics™ CRM Live is scheduled to be available in 2007. See press release at http://www.microsoft.com/presspass/press/2006/jul06/07-11CRMLivePR.mspx.
Special price breaks may be available to early adopters. Contact Microsoft for more information.
Blogs: http://thenorwichgroup.blogs.com/mscrm
Books: Working with Microsoft Dynamics™ CRM 3.0 by: Mike Snyder, Jim Steger; Microsoft CRM 3 For Dummies by: Joel Scott, David Lee; Special Edition Using Microsoft CRM by: Laura Brown, John Gravely
User Groups: Microsoft CRM Newsgroup (http://www.microsoft.com/Businesssolutions/Community/Newsgroups/dgbrowser/en-us/default.mspx?dg=microsoft.public.crm&lang=en&cr=US), MS CRM Study Group (http://finance.groups.yahoo.com/group/MSCRMStudy/), MS CRM User Group (http://groups.yahoo.com/group/mscrm_smb/)</td></tr>
</table>

EPM-1 Microsoft Office Project Screen Shot

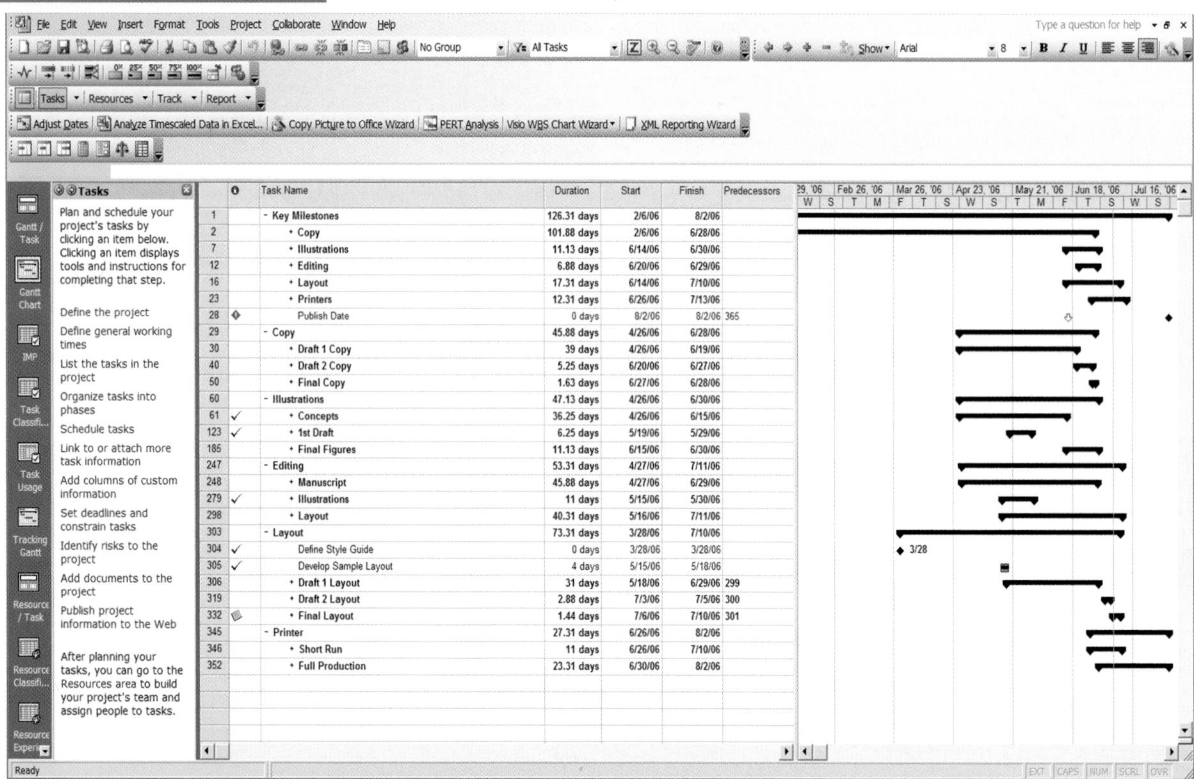

EPM-1 Microsoft Office Project Profile

<table>
<tr><th>Solution ID</th><th colspan="3">Solution Title</th><th colspan="2">Solution Provider</th><th colspan="2">Solution Category</th></tr>
<tr><td>EPM-1</td><td colspan="3">Microsoft Office Project</td><td colspan="2">Microsoft (www.microsoft.com)</td><td colspan="2">Enterprise Project Management</td></tr>
<tr><th colspan="8">Solution Description</th></tr>
<tr><td colspan="8">Project Standard 2003 helps project managers, business managers, and planners manage schedules and resources. Project Standard 2003 can help you set up projects quickly, communicate project data, and track and analyze projects (SOURCE: microsoft.com). Project Professional 2003 is required for use with Project Server 2003.</td></tr>
<tr><th colspan="8">Software</th></tr>
<tr><th>Title</th><th>Vendor</th><th colspan="4">Product Info</th><th colspan="2">Dependencies</th></tr>
<tr><td>Microsoft Office Project</td><td>Microsoft</td><td colspan="4">http://www.microsoft.com/office/project/prodinfo/default.mspx</td><td colspan="2">INF-1</td></tr>
<tr><th colspan="8">Costs</th></tr>
<tr><th colspan="4">Deployment Costs</th><th colspan="4">Operating Costs</th></tr>
<tr><th colspan="2">Labor Expenses</th><th colspan="2">Technology Expenses</th><th colspan="2">Labor Expenses</th><th colspan="2" rowspan="3">Technology Expenses</th></tr>
<tr><th rowspan="2">Task</th><th rowspan="2">Effort</th><th colspan="2">Software Licensing</th><th rowspan="2">Task</th><th rowspan="2">Effort</th></tr>
<tr><th>Cost</th><th>Type</th></tr>
<tr><td>**Installation**</td><td>Low</td><td rowspan="5">$599 for Standard
$999 for Professional</td><td rowspan="5">1 User
1 User</td><td>**Configuration Administration**</td><td>Low</td><td>**Upgrades**</td><td>Contact Microsoft partners about Software Assurance program benefits and eligibility.</td></tr>
<tr><td>**Configuration**</td><td>Low</td><td rowspan="4">**Technical Administration**</td><td rowspan="4">Low</td><td rowspan="4">**Incremental Users**</td><td rowspan="4">Contact Microsoft partners about Volume Licensing program.</td></tr>
<tr><td>**Customization**</td><td>NA</td></tr>
<tr><td>**Data Migration**</td><td>Low</td></tr>
<tr><td>**Training**</td><td>Medium</td></tr>
<tr><th colspan="8">More Information</th></tr>
<tr><td colspan="8">Microsoft Office Project comes with project guides that walk users through the process of developing and managing a project schedule.
The Microsoft Project Association (www.mpug.org) is an excellent resource for information on Microsoft Project from experienced users.
Project plan templates can be downloaded from microsoft.com free of charge.</td></tr>
</table>

EPM-2 Project Server Screen Shot

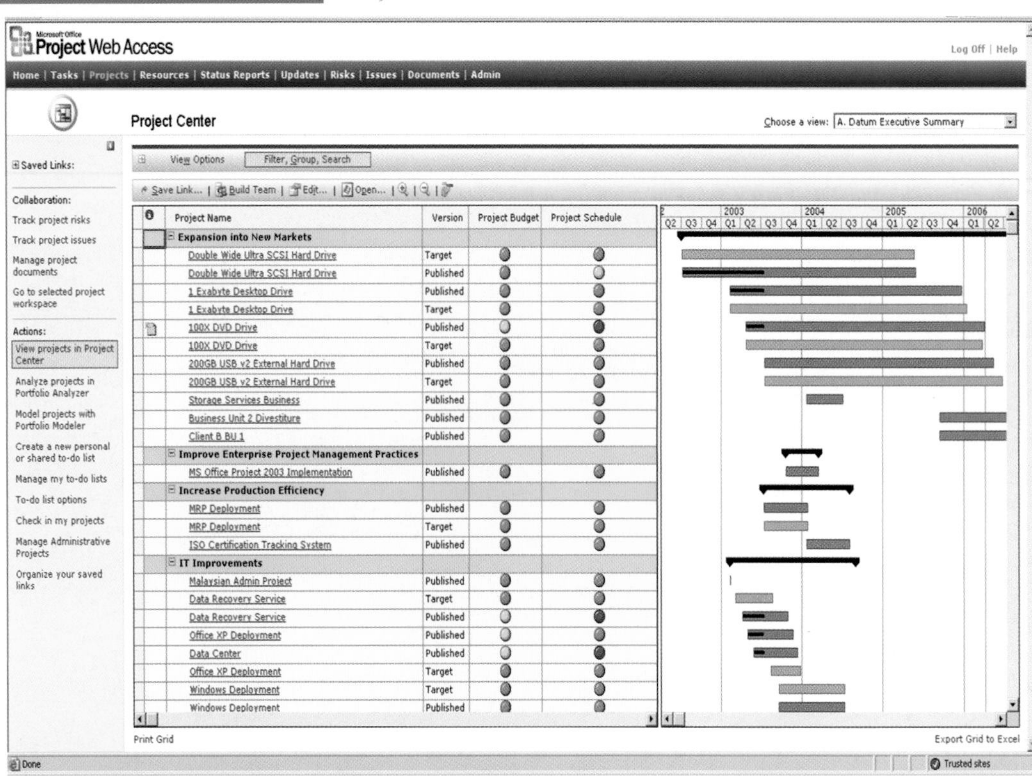

EPM-2 Project Server Profile

Solution ID	Solution Title	Solution Provider	Solution Category
EPM-2	Project Server	Microsoft (www.microsoft.com)	Enterprise Project Management

Solution Description

Project Server is a server-based supplement to the Microsoft Office Project client software that provides a central repository for project plan information. The centralized repository enables project managers, resource managers, resources, and executives to access virtual real-time project information including timing, costs, issues, risks, and project documentation all from within a web-based user interface.

Software

Title	Vendor	Product Info	Dependencies
Project Server	Microsoft	http://www.microsoft.com/office/project/prodinfo/epm/default.mspx	EPM-1 (Professional Edition), INF-2, INF-4

Costs

Deployment Costs				Operating Costs			
Labor Expenses		Technology Expenses		Labor Expenses		Technology Expenses	
Task	Effort	Software Licensing: Cost	Software Licensing: Type	Task	Effort		
Installation	Medium	$1,135	Server	Configuration Administration	High	Upgrades	License includes Software Assurance.coverage. See Microsoft Partner for details.
Configuration	Medium			Technical Administration	Low	Incremental Users	$67 per CAL without Software Assurance option. $200 per CAL with Software Assurance option.
Customization	NA						
Data Migration	Medium						
Training	High						

More Information

The Microsoft Project Association (www.mpug.org) is an excellent resource for information on Microsoft Project from experienced users.
Pcubed (www.pcubed.com) is a Microsoft Gold Certifed Partner that has deployed Project Server for hundreds of clients worldwide.
They have developed several customized solutions that supplement the core features of Project Server.

FIN-1 Small Business Accounting Screen Shot

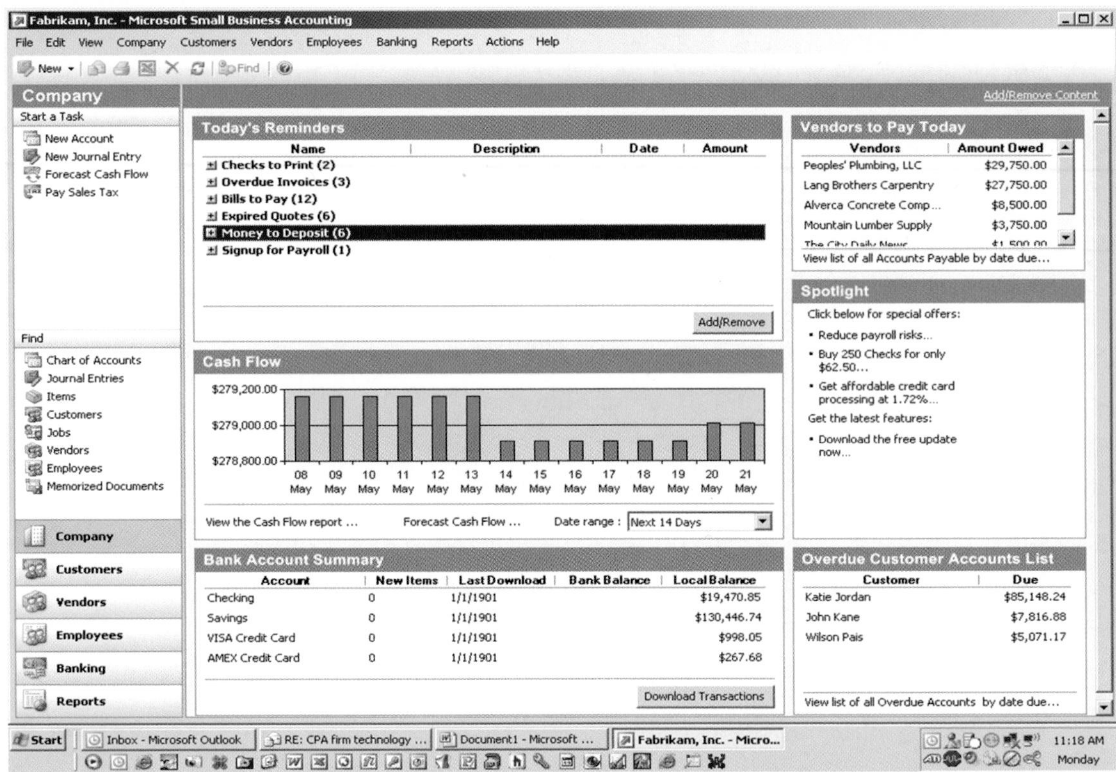

FIN-1 Small Business Accounting Profile

Solution ID	Solution Title	Solution Provider	Solution Category
FIN-1	Small Business Accounting	The Norwich Group (www.thenorwichgroup.com)	Financial Management

Solution Description

Small Business Accounting is a full-featured business management program that allows small business owners to manage their business financials using out-of-the-box software. This software includes the following capabilities: accounts receivable, accounts payable, general ledger, banking, credit card management, ADP payroll link, budgeting, inventory, time tracking, and an interface to Business Contact Manager running in Outlook 2003.

Software

Title	Vendor	Product Info	Dependencies
Small Business Accounting	Microsoft	http://www.microsoft.com/smallbusiness/products/office/accounting/detail.mspx	INF-1, COM-1 (OPTIONAL)

Costs

<table>
<tr><th colspan="4">Deployment Costs</th><th colspan="4">Operating Costs</th></tr>
<tr><th colspan="2">Labor Expenses</th><th colspan="2">Technology Expenses</th><th colspan="2">Labor Expenses</th><th colspan="2" rowspan="3">Technology Expenses</th></tr>
<tr><th rowspan="2">Task</th><th rowspan="2">Effort</th><th colspan="2">Software Licensing</th><th rowspan="2">Task</th><th rowspan="2">Effort</th></tr>
<tr><th>Cost</th><th>Type</th></tr>
<tr><td>Installation</td><td>Low</td><td rowspan="5">$125-$179</td><td rowspan="5">User</td><td>Configuration Administration</td><td>Low</td><td>Upgrades</td><td>Not specified (SBA 2006 is the first major release).</td></tr>
<tr><td>Configuration</td><td>Medium</td><td rowspan="4">Technical Administration</td><td rowspan="4">Low</td><td rowspan="4">Incremental Users</td><td rowspan="4">$125-$179 per user. Contact Microsoft Authorized Reseller for latest incentive offers.</td></tr>
<tr><td>Customization</td><td>NA</td></tr>
<tr><td>Data Migration</td><td>High</td></tr>
<tr><td>Training</td><td>Medium</td></tr>
</table>

More Information

The following add-on services are available: Payroll, Credit Card Processing, Checks & Forms.
See http://www.microsoft.com/smallbusiness/products/office/accounting/small-business-accounting-services.mspx for more details.
The Microsoft Office team has offered to provide free training.
Websites: Microsoft SBA Website (http://sba.microsoft.com/),
Blogs: SBA Blog (https://blogs.msdn.com/rajattaneja/default.aspx)
Books: *Microsoft Office Small Business Accounting 2006 Step by Step* by Fred Curtis
Articles: http://office.microsoft.com/en-us/assistance/HA100964131033.aspx
User Groups: http://finance.groups.yahoo.com/group/MS_SBA/

FIN-2 Small Business Financials Screen Shot

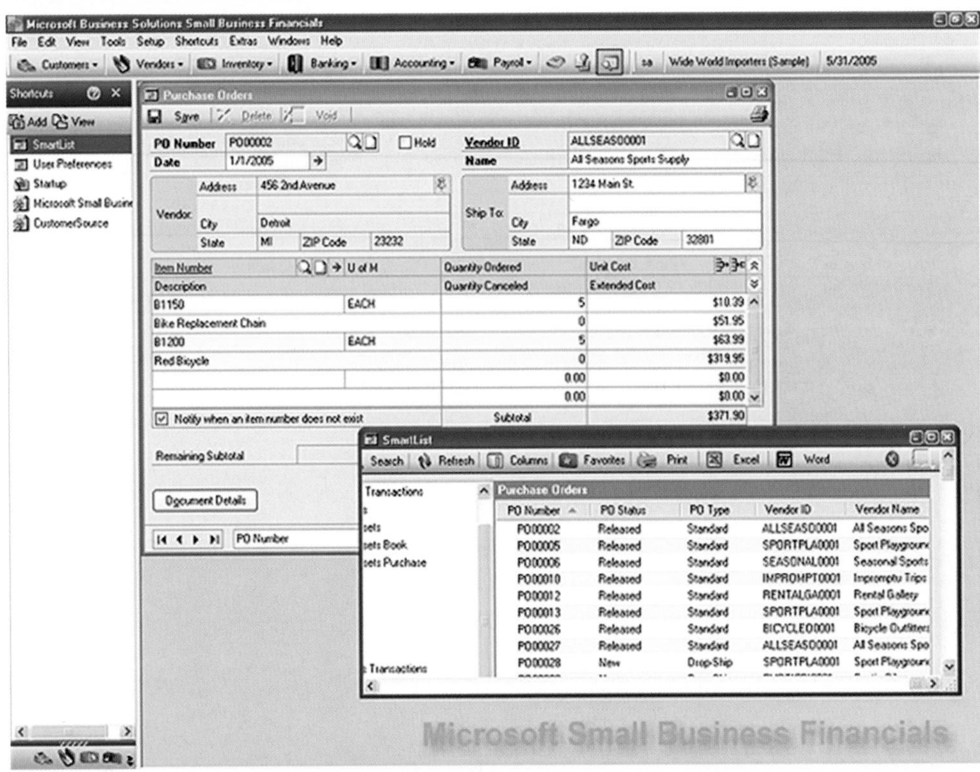

FIN-2 Small Business Financials Profile

Solution ID	Solution Title	Solution Provider	Solution Category
FIN-2	Small Business Financials	Microsoft (www.microsoft.com)	Financial Management

Solution Description

For companies that have outgrown basic accounting applications, this business solution offers functionality to better manage financials, sales, purchasing, inventory, payroll, reporting, and more. With Microsoft Small Business Financials, you can process transactions more efficiently; get a comprehensive view of information across your business; and manage the complete customer, vendor, and product life cycle—all in one application (SOURCE: microsoft.com).

Software

Title	Vendor	Product Info	Dependencies
Small Business Financials	Microsoft	http://www.microsoft.com/businesssolutions/smallbusinessfinancials/default.mspx	INF-2, INF-4

Costs

Deployment Costs				Operating Costs			
Labor Expenses		Technology Expenses		Labor Expenses		Technology Expenses	
		Software Licensing					
Task	Effort	Cost	Type	Task	Effort		
Installation	Medium	Contact a Microsoft Solution Partner for solution-based pricing	Varies by configuration	**Configuration Administration**	High	**Upgrades**	Contact Microsoft partners about Software Assurance program benefits and eligibility.
Configuration	High			**Technical Administration**	Medium	**Incremental Users**	Contact Microsoft partners about Volume Licensing program.
Customization	NA						
Data Migration	High						
Training	Medium						

More Information

You can find Microsoft Partners near you to help you deploy solutions for your business at https://www.microsoft.com/smallbusiness/products/solution-advisor.mspx. Small Business Financials is a derivative of the Microsoft Dynamics GP (Great Plains) product intended for businesses with less than 75 employees.

INF-1 Windows XP Screen Shot

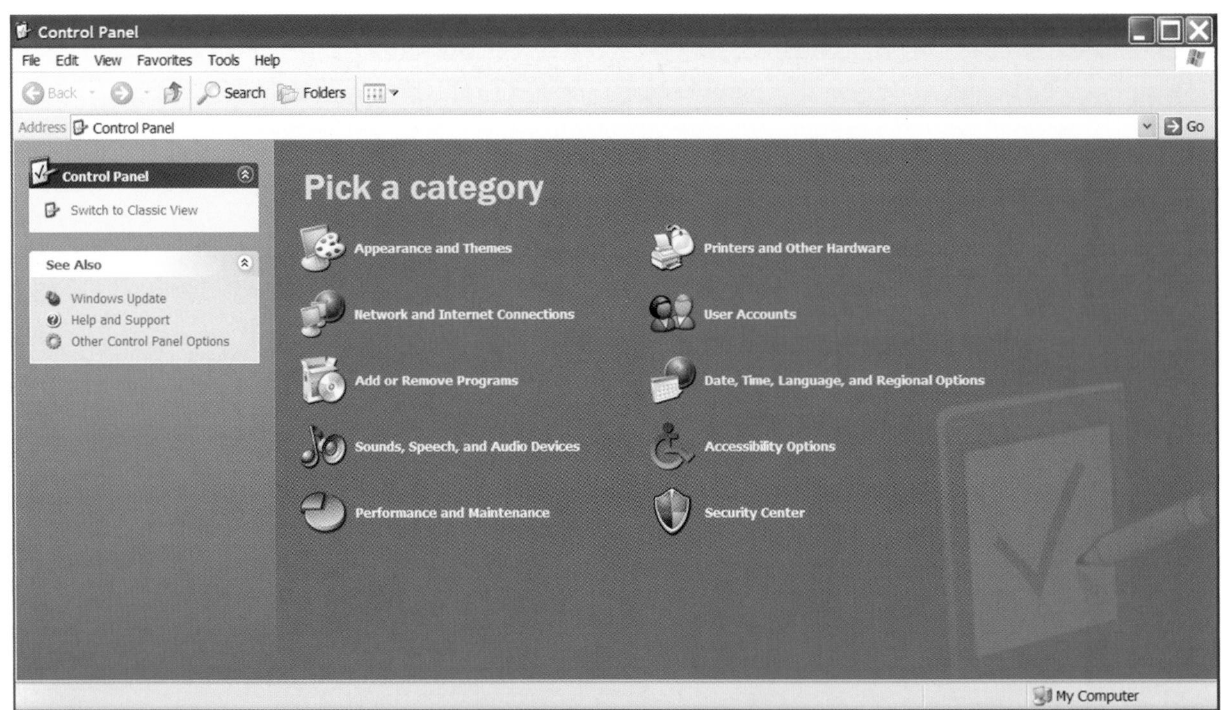

INF-1 Windows XP Profile

Solution ID	Solution Title	Solution Provider	Solution Category
INF-1	Windows XP	Microsoft (www.microsoft.com)	Infrastructure

Solution Description

Windows XP Professional gives your small business the dependability you need to get more done with less effort and stay better connected with customers and business partners. With improved networking tools, advanced security settings and recovery options, it sets a new standard for a foundation you can count on to keep your desktop or notebook computer up and running.
(SOURCE: microsoft.com)

Software

Title	Vendor	Product Info	Dependencies
Windows XP	Microsoft	http://www.microsoft.com/windowsxp/default.mspx	NA

Costs

Deployment Costs

Labor Expenses: Task	Labor Expenses: Effort	Technology Expenses – Software Licensing: Cost	Technology Expenses – Software Licensing: Type
Installation	Low	$115-$280 (Significant variation depending upon vendor)	User
Configuration	Low		
Customization	NA		
Data Migration	Low		
Training	Low		

Operating Costs

Labor Expenses: Task	Labor Expenses: Effort	Technology Expenses	
Configuration Administration	Low	**Upgrades**	Software Assurance Program available.
Technical Administration	Low	**Incremental Users**	Volume discounts available. See Authorized Reseller for latest incentives.

More Information

Windows Vista is the next generation of Windows XP. It is projected to be available for purchase in 2007.

INF-2 Windows Server Screen Shot

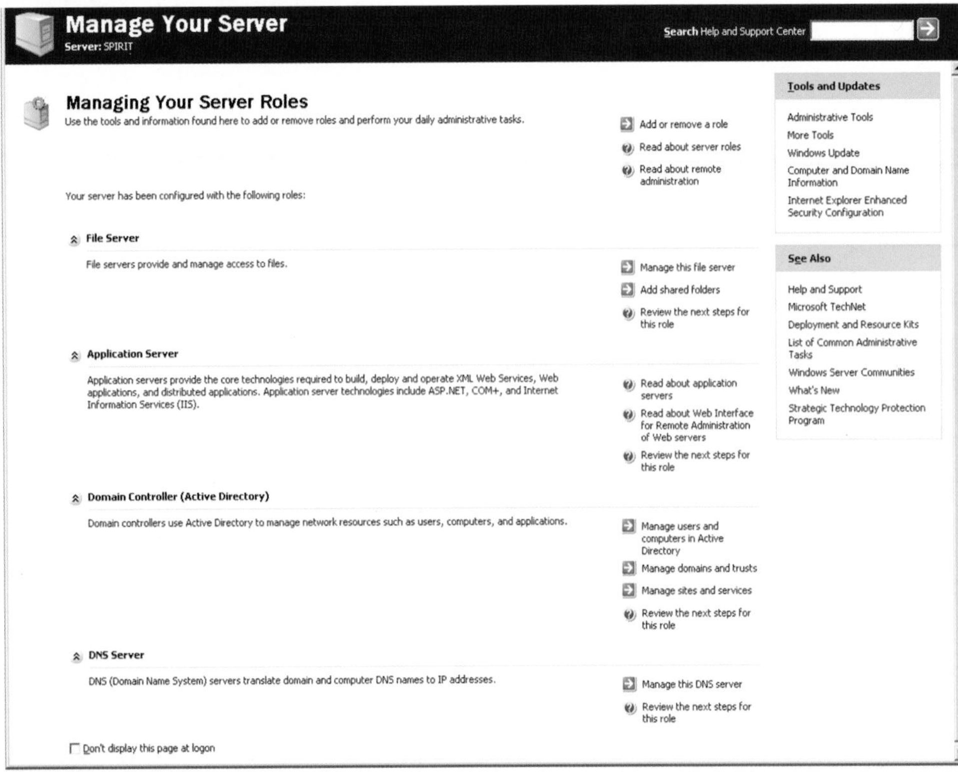

INF-2 Windows Server Profile

<table>
<tr><th>Solution ID</th><th colspan="3">Solution Title</th><th colspan="2">Solution Provider</th><th colspan="2">Solution Category</th></tr>
<tr><td>INF-2</td><td colspan="3">Windows Server</td><td colspan="2">Microsoft (www.microsoft.com)</td><td colspan="2">Infrastructure</td></tr>
<tr><th colspan="8">Solution Description</th></tr>
<tr><td colspan="8">Windows Server 2003 is the most productive infrastructure platform for powering connected applications, networks, and Web services from the workgroup to the data center. Easy to deploy, manage, and use, Windows Server 2003 helps you build a secure IT infrastructure that provides a powerful application platform for quickly building connected solutions and an information worker infrastructure for enhanced communication and collaboration anytime and anywhere (SOURCE: microsoft.com).</td></tr>
<tr><th colspan="8">Software</th></tr>
<tr><th>Title</th><th>Vendor</th><th colspan="4">Product Info</th><th colspan="2">Dependencies</th></tr>
<tr><td>Windows Server</td><td>Microsoft</td><td colspan="4">http://www.microsoft.com/windowsserver2003/default.mspx</td><td colspan="2">NA</td></tr>
<tr><th colspan="8">Costs</th></tr>
<tr><th colspan="4">Deployment Costs</th><th colspan="4">Operating Costs</th></tr>
<tr><th colspan="2">Labor Expenses</th><th colspan="2">Technology Expenses</th><th colspan="2">Labor Expenses</th><th colspan="2" rowspan="3">Technology Expenses</th></tr>
<tr><th rowspan="2">Task</th><th rowspan="2">Effort</th><th colspan="2">Software Licensing</th><th rowspan="2">Task</th><th rowspan="2">Effort</th></tr>
<tr><th>Cost</th><th>Type</th></tr>
<tr><td>Installation</td><td>Medium</td><td rowspan="5">$1,199 for Standard Edition
$3,999 for Enterprise Edition
(SOURCE: microsoft.com)</td><td rowspan="5">1 Server plus 10 CAL's
1 Server plus 25 CAL's</td><td>Configuration Administration</td><td>Low</td><td>Upgrades</td><td>Contact Microsoft partners about Software Assurance program benefits and eligibility.</td></tr>
<tr><td>Configuration</td><td>Medium</td><td rowspan="4">Technical Administration</td><td rowspan="4">Low</td><td rowspan="4">Incremental Users</td><td rowspan="4">$199 for 5 CAL's
$799 for 20 CAL's</td></tr>
<tr><td>Customization</td><td>NA</td></tr>
<tr><td>Data Migration</td><td>Low</td></tr>
<tr><td>Training</td><td>Low</td></tr>
<tr><th colspan="8">More Information</th></tr>
<tr><td colspan="8">Windows Server is the server equivalent to the popular Windows XP operating system for desktop (client) computers.
You can find Microsoft Partners near you to help you deploy solutions for your business at https://www.microsoft.com/smallbusiness/products/solution-advisor.mspx.</td></tr>
</table>

INF-3 Small Business Server Screen Shot

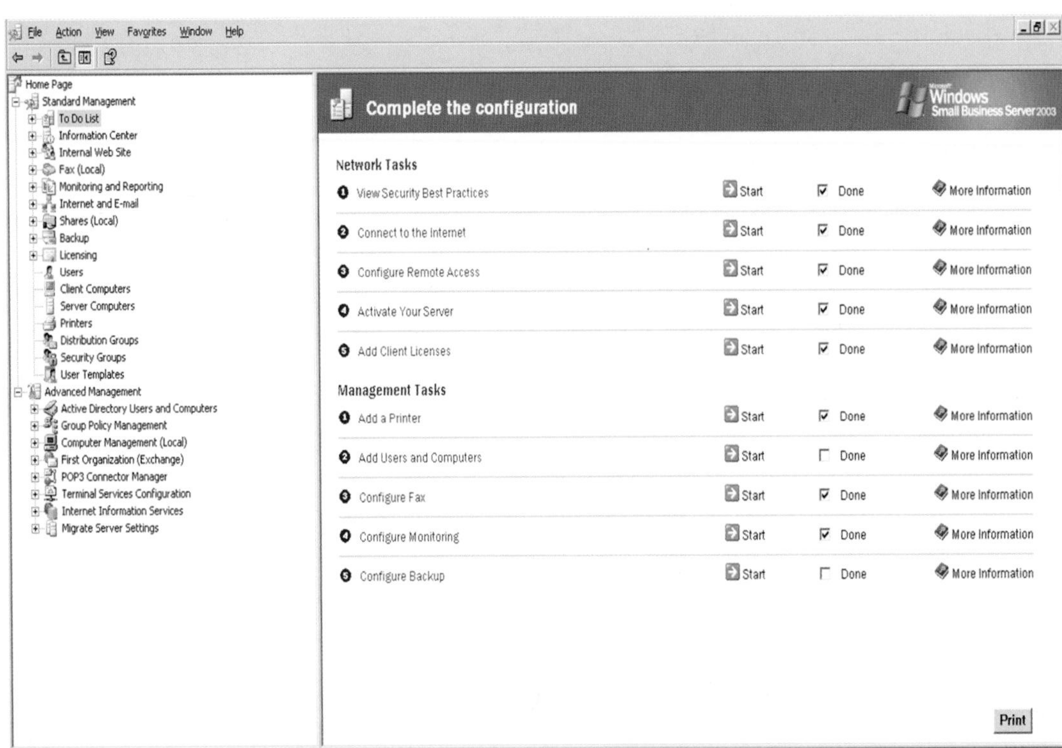

INF-3 Small Business Server Profile

Solution ID	Solution Title	Solution Provider	Solution Category
INF-3	Small Business Server	Microsoft (www.microsoft.com)	Infrastructure

Solution Description

Today's small businesses are challenged to do things better, faster, and with fewer resources. Windows Small Business Server 2003 provides technologies and tools (including Windows SharePoint Services collaboration tool) to help small businesses become more productive and efficient, including e-mail, shared documents and calendars, security-enhanced Internet access and data storage, reliable printing and faxing, and remote administration.
Windows Small Business Server 2003 is available in two editions: standard and premium. (SOURCE: microsoft.com)

Software

Title	Vendor	Product Info	Dependencies
Small Business Server	Microsoft	http://www.microsoft.com/windowsserver2003/sbs/default.mspx	Works best with INF-1 and COM-1

Costs

Deployment Costs				Operating Costs			
Labor Expenses		Technology Expenses		Labor Expenses		Technology Expenses	
		Software Licensing[2]					
Task	Effort	Cost	Type	Task	Effort		
Installation	Medium	$599 for Standard Edition $1,499 for Premium Edition (SOURCE: microsoft.com)	Server plus 5 CAL's for either edition	**Configuration Administration**	Medium	**Upgrades**	Contact Microsoft partners about Software Assurance program benefits and eligibility.
Configuration	Medium			**Technical Administration**	Medium	**Incremental Users**	$489 for 5 more users $1,929 for 20 more users
Customization	Low						
Data Migration	Low						
Training	Low						

More Information

SMB Nation (www.smbnation.com) provides excellent resources for getting you in touch with experts on Small Business Server.
Microsoft has a Small Business Center website (http://www.microsoft.com/smallbusiness/hub.mspx) that provides excellent information pertinent to technology concerns of small businesses. You can find Microsoft Partners near you to help you deploy solutions for your business at https://www.microsoft.com/smallbusiness/products/solution-advisor.mspx.

[2] *Source of pricing figures is http://www.microsoft.com/windowsserver2003/sbs/howtobuy/pricing.mspx effective June 24, 2006*

INF-4 SQL Server Screen Shot

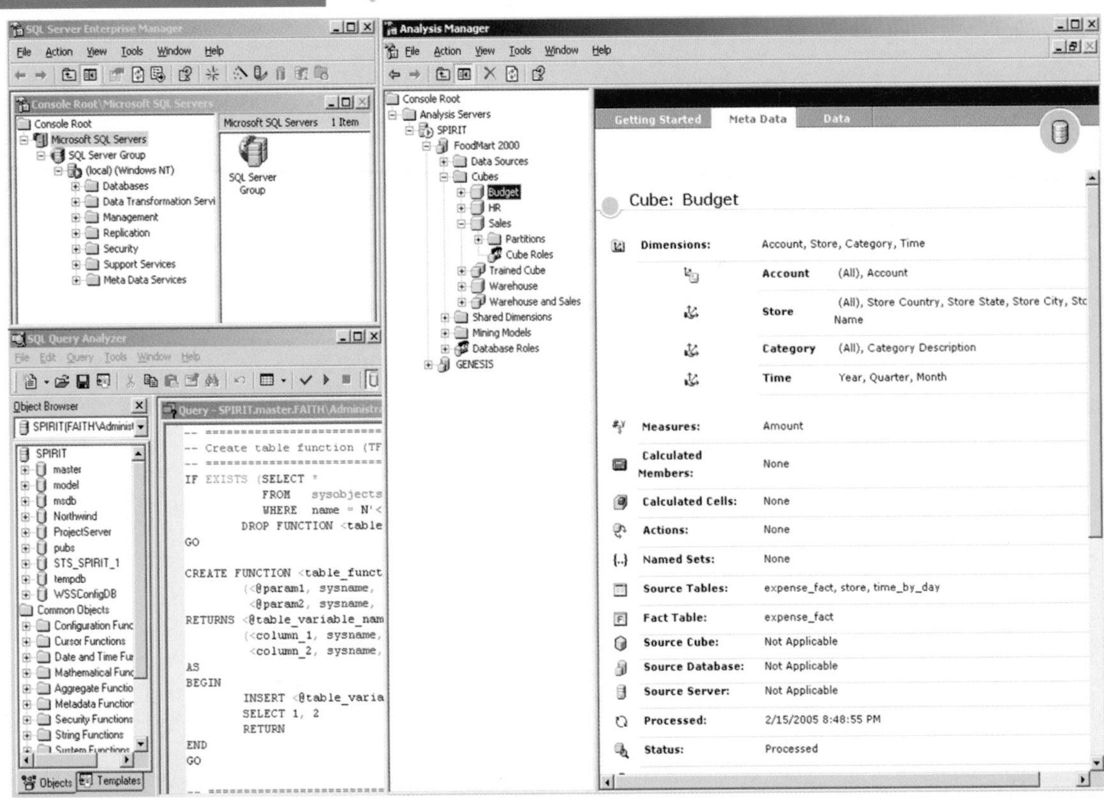

INF-4 SQL Server Profile

Solution ID	Solution Title	Solution Provider	Solution Category
INF-4	SQL Server	Microsoft (www.microsoft.com)	Infrastructure

Solution Description
SQL Server 2005 is a comprehensive database platform providing enterprise-class data management with integrated business intelligence (BI) tools. The SQL Server 2005 database engine provides more secure, reliable storage for both relational and structured data, enabling you to build and manage highly available, performant data applications that you and your people can use to take your business to the next level (SOURCE: microsoft.com).

Software			
Title	**Vendor**	**Product Info**	**Dependencies**
SQL Server	Microsoft	http://www.microsoft.com/sql/default.mspx	INF-2

Costs								
Deployment Costs				**Operating Costs**				
Labor Expenses		**Technology Expenses**		**Labor Expenses**		**Technology Expenses**		
Task	**Effort**	**Software Licensing**		**Task**	**Effort**			
		Cost	**Type**					
Installation	Medium	$13,819 for Enterprise Edition (SOURCE: microsoft.com)	1 Server and 25 Clients	**Configuration Administration**	Medium	**Upgrades**	Contact Microsoft partners about Software Assurance program benefits and eligibility.	
Configuration	Medium			**Technical Administration**	Medium	**Incremental Users**	Contact Microsoft partners about Volume Licensing program.	
Customization	NA							
Data Migration	High							
Training	Medium							

More Information
Most advanced software solutions based on the Microsoft platform depend upon SQL server to manage their data. You can find Microsoft Partners near you to help you deploy solutions for your business at https://www.microsoft.com/smallbusiness/products/solution-advisor.mspx.

APPENDIX 2: POCKET IT ROADMAP CONSTRUCTION GUIDE

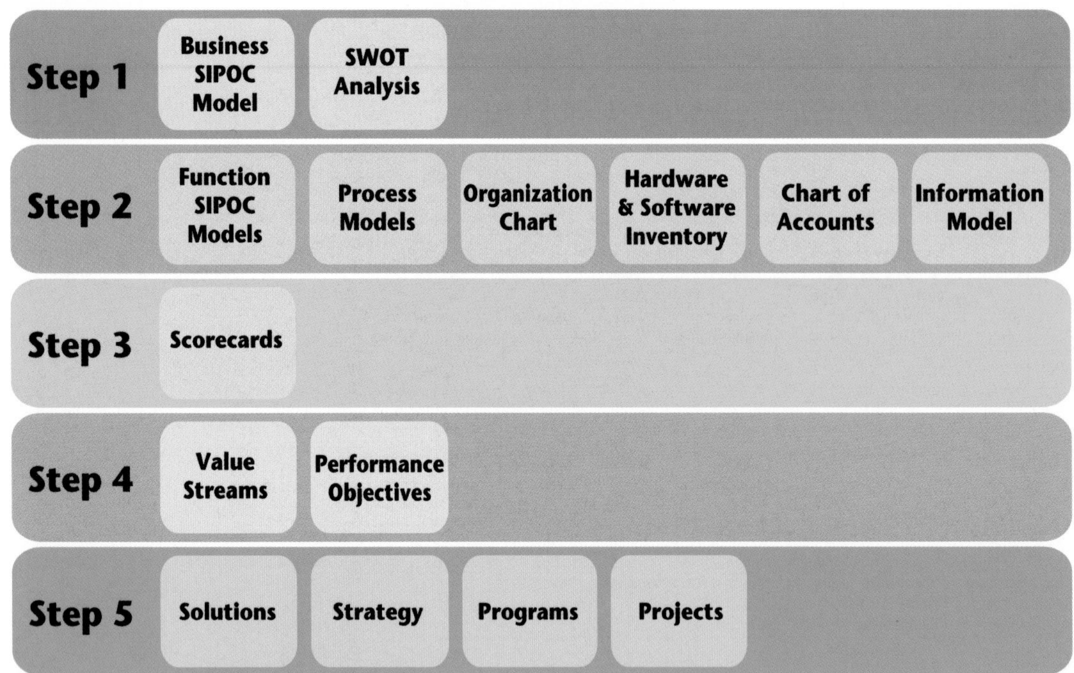

APPENDIX 3: SMALL BUSINESS RESOURCES

Resource	Description	How to access resource?
Perspective Shifts, LLC	Microsoft Small Business Specialist services firm that can help you map out your personal IT Roadmap.	www.perspectiveshifts.biz
Pocket Consultant Series	Website sponsored by PerspectiveShifts, LLC featuring information and tools that supplement the Pocket Consultant Series of books.	www.pocketconsultantseries.com
SMB Nation	SMB Nation provides global small and medium business resources for technology channel partners, consultants, resellers, system builders and all small business technology professionals seeking to improve their professionalism and better serve their end-user customers.	www.smbnation.com
Startup Nation	Forum providing expert advice on topics of interest to entrepreneurs.	www.startupnation.com
Microsoft Small Business Center	Microsoft-sponsored portal that provides small businesses with access to personalized training and support resources.	http://www.microsoft.com/smallbusiness/hub.mspx
Microsoft Solution Builder	Online assessment tool provided by Microsoft to identify the computer technology that your business needs.	http://www.microsoft.com/smallbusiness/partner/computer-builder.mspx
Microsoft Professional Services Site	Microsoft website featuring case studies, solutions, and value propositions specific to Professional Service Firms.	http://www.microsoft.com/industry/professionalservices/default.mspx
Microsoft Financing	Microsoft financing program designed to help small businesses afford advanced solutions for their business.	http://www.microsoft.com/licensing/financing/default.mspx
Computer Troubleshooters	Computer Troubleshooters provides businesses and homes with IT support services.	http://www.computertroubleshooters.com/

Glossary

Architecture: The description of a system of components, how these components relate to one another and how they interact with each other. Software architecture diagrams feature software programs. Physical architecture diagrams typically feature hardware devices.

Application: Alternate term for software program (e.g. Microsoft Outlook).

Blog: Short for "Weblog", it refers to a serial newsletter delivered via the internet on a particular subject.

Business Case: A worksheet comparing the benefits and costs for a given business strategy or program.

Business Model: A manner of representing business operations that can be used to predict the financial performance of the business and analyze business strategy. A business model can be represented as a group of resource-loaded process models.

Charter: A document that defines the overall scope and direction for an activity.

Client: A desktop PC or laptop that accesses the information on a server in a client-server network.

Client-Server Network: A client-server network with internet access is the current model for an advanced network. Information access by clients is controlled by a centralized server. The client-server network provides businesses with the most security, flexibility, and scalability.

Dashboard: A read-only collection of metrics or KPI's that can be used to monitor business performance. Typically, dashboards are web-based programs that can be viewed in your web browser (e.g. Internet Explorer).

Extranet: The extension of a local area network (LAN) or intranet across an external infrastructure (e.g. internet, phone line) to provide remote users with a secure means of accessing data or applications on their LAN.

Firewall: Hardware or software that restricts the flow of information into and out of your network.

Hub: Hardware device used to connect multiple devices on a network.

Infrastructure: The collection of hardware (e.g. servers, hubs, modems) and utility software (e.g. operating systems, database applications, firewalls) that provides end users with the ability to share information across a network.

Internet: A worldwide network of computers that shares information in accordance with established protocols.

Intranet: The internal network for an organization that allows the sharing of information between a select group of users and computers. If the intranet is connected to the internet, the intranet is typically protected by a firewall that limits traffic to and from the internet.

KPI: Short for Key Performance Indicator. KPI's are metrics that describe the performance of an organization (e.g. Revenue, Expenses).

Operations: The execution of functional process models in a manner that reflects the basic "day in the life" of your organization.

Peer-to-Peer Network: The sharing of information between computers without a server. Computers are connected via cables or wirelessly. Cabling connections often include the use of a hub or router, but not a connection to a centralized server.

Performance Gap: The difference between your current performance and your desired performance.

Process Model: Diagram depicting the standard sequence of tasks executed by one or more organizations. In the process models shown in this book, rectangular blocks represent tasks, block arrows depict triggering events, and diamonds represent decision points.

Program: Programs are a group of projects organized around a common goal (e.g. value stream objectives).

Project: Projects are groups of activities defined to implement a specific objective or set thereof within a specified period of time using a finite set of resources. IT projects typically feature the deployment of a solution to a specific group of users.

Resource: Someone or something that executes a task within a process or project.

Roadmap: A success-oriented plan that will enable you to implement your business strategy.

Router: Hardware device used to route information between devices on a network.

Scorecard: A select group of key performance indicators.

Server: A computer that provides information for one or more client computers on a client-server network.

Service Level Agreement: Contract between service provider and customer that documents service expectations (e.g. system availability, issue response times).

SIPOC Model: Short for Suppliers, Inputs, Processes, Outputs, and Customers. Typically used as a high-level model of information flow.

Sneakernet: A slang term for a network without any physical or wireless connections between computers. Files are transferred via floppy disks, CD-Roms, flash drives or the like.

Solution: Solutions are systems of software, services and hardware that enable organizations to fill gaps between their desired performance and their current performance (i.e. solve a problem).

Specification: A refinement of the scope defined in a Charter to reflect specific functions or features that are required by a solution (requirements specification) or reflected in a solution (design specification).

Statement of Work: A contractual document outlining the deliverable requirements associated with a given scope of work. Often abbreviated as SOW.

SWOT Analysis: Short for Strengths, Weaknesses, Opportunities, and Threats. SWOT analyses provide high-level assessments of a business model.

Task: The lowest level of granularity used for describing an activity in a process model or project plan. Resources are assigned to tasks to estimate and track costs for the activity.

Technology: Hardware or software tools designed to help people execute their job more effectively.

Value Stream: A select group of tasks that heavily influence the performance of one or more areas of your business. The purpose of value streams is to provide you with a quick method of evaluating the benefit of pursuing a certain business improvement strategy.

Index

List of Figures

List of Tables

References

BOOKS

Boorstin, Daniel J. *The Discoverers.* First Ed. New York: Random House, 1983. 745 pp.

Brelsford, Harry. *Advanced Windows Small Business Server 2003 Best Practices.* SMB Nation Press, 2005. 1,075 pp.

Hagel, John, III. *Out of the Box: Strategies for Achieving Profits Today and Growth Tomorrow through Web Services.* Boston: Harvard Business School Press, 2002. 217 pp.

Heiman, Richard V. and Dennis Byron. *IDC's Software Taxonomy, 2005.* IDC, 2005. 93 pp. Adobe Acrobat e-book.

Kaye, Doug. *Loosely Coupled: The Missing Pieces of Web Services.* Marin County, CA: RDS Press, 2003. 334 pp.

Lah, Thomas E., et. al. *Building Professional Services: The Sirens' Song.* Upper Saddle River, NJ: Prentice Hall PTR, 2002. 360 pp.

Owen, Anerin Sion. *Accounting for Business Studies.* Butterworth-Heinemann, 2003. 440 pp.

Russel, Charlie, et. al. *Microsoft Windows Small Business Server 2003 Administrator's Companion.* Redmond, WA: Microsoft Press.

Scheer, August-Wilhelm. *Business Process Engineering: Reference Models for Industrial Enterprises.* New York: Springer, 1998. 757 pp.

Smith, Adam. *The Wealth of Nations* (Edwin Cannan, ed.). New York: Bantam Classic, 2003. 1231 pp.

Tapping, Don, Tom Luyster and Tom Shuker. *Value Stream Management: Eight Steps to Planning, Mapping, and Sustaining Lean Improvements.* New York: Productivity, 2002. 169 pp.

PERIODICALS

Koch, Christopher. "The Metrics Trap...And How to Avoid It." *CIO* Magazine. 1 April 2006. http://www.cio.com/archive/040106/metrics.html

ONLINE REFERENCES

"Are Fees Tax Deductable?" Recruiting Life Industry Forum. http://www.recruitinglife.com/forum/printthread.cfm?Forum=6&Topic=27 (accessed July 15, 2006).

Balanced Scorecard Institute. www.balancedscorecard.org.

"How to Buy Microsoft Office Business Scorecard Manager 2005." Microsoft Corporation. http://office.microsoft.com/en-us/assistance/HA100621061033.aspx (accessed July 15, 2006).

"Live Meeting: Buy It." Microsoft Corporation. http://main.placeware.com/ordering/lmbuy_it/buy_it.cfm?promocode=2730 (accessed July 15, 2006).

"Live Meeting Frequently Asked Questions." Microsoft Corporation. http://www.microsoft.com/office/livemeeting/prodinfo/faq.mspx (accessed July 15, 2006).

"Live Meeting: How to Buy." Microsoft Corporation. http://www.microsoft.com/office/livemeeting/howtobuy/default.mspx (accessed July 15, 2006).

"Now your PCs Can Work as Hard as You." Microsoft Corporation. http://www.microsoft.com/windowsxp/business/default.mspx (accessed July 15, 2006).

"Paradigm Shift." Recruiting Life Industry Forum. http://www.recruitinglife.com/forum/printthread.cfm?Forum=6&Topic=1 (accessed July 15, 2006).

"**Product Information: Microsoft Windows XP Professional (SP2)**" eDirectSoftware. https://shop.edirectsoftware.com/catalog/product_info.php?products_id=16134 (accessed July 15, 2006).

"**Small Business Accounting 2006 Comparison Chart.**" Microsoft Corporation. http://www.microsoft.com/office/accounting/prodinfo/quickcompare.mspx (accessed July 15, 2006).

"**Small Business Accounting Add in Services.**" Microsoft Corporation. http://www.microsoft.com/smallbusiness/products/office/accounting/small-business-accounting-services.mspx (accessed July 15, 2006).

"**Software Buying Options from Microsoft Small Business.**" Microsoft Corporation. http://www.microsoft.com/smallbusiness/buy/software/options.mspx.\ (accessed July 15, 2006).

INDUSTRY STANDARDS

Institute of Electrical and Electronics Engineers, Inc. Standard 1498.

About the Author

Patrick J. Colbeck has over 10 years of experience providing consulting services as a member of the Professional Services industry. In 2004, he founded Perspective Shifts, LLC, as a means to help clients improve the connection between business operations and the projects intended to improve those operations. During his career, he has provided consulting services to clients in a wide variety of industries, including Professional Services, Aerospace, Defense, Automotive, Telecommunications, Investment Banking, Pharmaceutical, and Healthcare. His breadth of experience has provided him with unique insights into what works and what doesn't work within today's business environment.

Mr. Colbeck has been certified by Microsoft as a Small Business Specialist. Among his professional accomplishments is the receipt of the Best Professional Services Automation Solution Award at the 2002 Microsoft Business Value Challenge.

His formal education includes Bachelors and Masters of Science degrees in Aerospace Engineering from the University of Michigan. He is also a graduate of the International Space University in Strasbourg, France. Mr. Colbeck lives with his wife Angie and dog Rastro in Canton, Michigan.

Notes

Notes

Notes

Notes

Notes

Notes

Notes

Notes